If You Only Knew

If You Only Knew

Navigating
DNA Surprises
and the
*NPE (Not-Parent Expected) World

Lezlee Liljenberg
CIC, CRIS, MLIS, MA, PA

ISBN (paperback): 979-8-9889597-0-0
ISBN (ebook): 979-8-9889597-1-7

Book design and production by www.AuthorSuccess.com

Printed in the United States of America

For Magnus, my Forever Love.

Thank you for being on this Journey called Life with me.

You make the good times Great
& the Tough Times Tolerable!

Contents

Preface

I am thrilled you are joining me on this Journey of DNA discovery. This book is a cross between real-life "Mama Mia" moments, a Lifetime movie, and a Hallmark show.

Have you ever looked in the mirror and wondered where your eyes or nose came from? Or question why you don't look like the other people in your family? These are age-old questions.

However, with DNA testing many people are finally getting answers. At times these answers are Welcomed, but for others it creates a "Life Interrupted" scenario. I happen to be one of those Life Interrupted people and the reason I am here to share this story.

First and foremost, I am an author, artist, and a Not-Parent Expected. An NPE is usually an adult, who through DNA testing has discovered at least one assumed parent is not his or her biological parent.

This book shares the experiences of my DNA Surprise, Discovery, Research, and personal Journey. There is one tremendous and explosive realization resulting from my NPE breakthrough though. NPEs are The New Minority!

What in the hell do you mean by that, Lezlee?

Let me explain. What I mean is we are a population that has been newly created by the DNA testing world. A minority is presented when a distinct group coexists but is subordinate to a more dominant group. In this instance NPE versus Non-NPE. According to

Britannica, minority status does not necessarily correlate to population but rather the significant distinguishing characteristics of the group. In this world of inclusion, acceptance, and diversity, this is an entirely unique culture: a culture that crosses all genders, races, religions, colors, and nationalities. There is no place for discrimination in this community because we are all equally confused and seeking the same outcome.

As a journalist, it has always been embedded in my head to search for the truth and not embellish the outcomes. There are a few fantasy chapters from my crazy brain included in this book. Other than those few chapters everything written here are absolute facts of my encounters during this adventure.

My Birth Certificate Father never turned his back on me and to this day tells me "I love you and I always have since the day you were born."

There are days when disappointment in my mother clinches my heart, but I remind myself what an amazing and loving mother she was to me. I would never change our relationship and what we had in a million years.

Has the deception hurt and on days been hard to absorb? Absolutely! But without understanding and being willing to accept the circumstances of how, why, and when they happened, I would just become a bitter spectator in my own life. I am not that girl! So, I chose to continue to learn and to forgive.

In approaching the matter with forgiveness and compassion, it became apparent this book about the NPE world was needed. If you are an NPE, holding someone's hand through the surprise or you have decided to be a person evading the facts placed in front of your very eyes this book is for you. Appreciation will never be a strong enough word to explain the deep feelings and emotions for those siblings, cousins, parents, aunts, uncles, and friends that walk this walk with us.

Like so many journeys you can never know how one feels until you walk in their shoes. The NPE is no different than others seeking equality for their sisters and brothers experiencing the same injustices. Most of us are working on coming to terms with the hand God dealt us.

The names of the players have been changed to protect the innocent in this little excursion of life.

The others, which are not so innocent, also have pseudonyms. Not to protect them but to protect me from any further retaliation. You know who you are!

Let me make one thing very clear in your perception of the NPE. None of us (or a miniscule few) are "out for something," or have some ulterior motive in mind. We just want help finding our way on a path stolen from us and kept from us through life until our DNA results revealed the discrepancies.

Try to unbundle your misgivings or insecurities and help open the doors that NPEs so sincerely crave. Anyone interviewed had the option to reveal their identities or to keep it private. Big thanks to all of those that shared their stories and offered more legitimacy and substance to the NPE universe.

Never heard of us? Well, sit back and enjoy the stories and the guidance offered to NPEs, the innocent (and not so innocent) bystanders, handholders and fellow voyagers.

I am a better person by going through this journey and hopefully this book can create peace for many others. In reading this book and realizing that "this shit is real," I encourage everyone to open their hearts and minds. I hope and pray this information helps those who have chosen to remain ignorant in an ever-changing cycle of life. Maybe this is a first step to recovery for many.

Glossary of Common Terms, Abbreviations, Acronyms and Phrases

As you move through this book, this glossary should prove helpful in deciphering the language of the NPE Universe. It is placed at the beginning for you to easily reference to it for clarification.

AC—Assisted Conception (egg/embryo/surrogacy/sperm donation)

AID—Artificial insemination by donor

ART—Artificial/assisted reproductive technology

BC—Birth certificate

BF—Birth father

BM—Birth mother

BCF—Birth certificate father

BCM—Birth certificate mother

BRW—Brother raised with

Biosplaining—"For people who don't have a clue telling us how we should feel" (Marianne Senechal)

Bruncle—Brother/uncle

CM—Centimorgans—CMs measure the distance in DNA to someone. The higher the CMs, the closer to a generational match.

DC—Donor conceived

DTD—Do the deed

FIL—father-in-law

FOB—Father of baby

FRM—Father raised me

FOMO—Fear of missing out

HB/HS—Half-brother/Half-sister

IUI—Intrauterine insemination-Internal artificial insemination

IVF—In vitro fertilization

LDA—Late Discovery Adoptee

MIL—Mother-in-law

MRM—Mother raised me

MPE—Misattributed parental event

NDB—Newly discovered brother

NDS—Newly discovered sister

NPE—Nonpaternal event, not-parent expected

POC—Products of conception

SFN—Stepfather name

SMN—stepmother name

SRW—Sister raised with

Introduction

Thumpity Thump, Thumpity Thump

My heart is pounding so hard against my chest I can barely breath. I am opening my second DNA results and am very well aware it will reveal secrets of my life and those of many others.

Ba Bump, Ba Bump, Ba Bump my heart beats ever faster when I see right before my eyes the words "Half-Sibling." There it is!! The proof I have been seeking for years and the answer to questions I have been asking myself and others for a lifetime it seems. There was another family out there I never had the privilege to know, and they were clueless that I even existed.

Thumpity Thump, ThumpityThump.

Once again, my heart races as I pick up the phone to dial the number of my half-sister for the first time. My prayer is she will accept me and the situation, but my hopes are dashed as I hear the contempt, anger, and accusations. Well, how rude!

This was the Moment of Truth when I knew in my soul there had to be others out there struggling with this same Not-Parent Expected (NPE) phenomenon. There just had to be more kindness and answers than what this person was willing to provide—Bye Felicia!

It was through these exact moments of pure relief and utter rejection I realized, pounding heart and all, this book needed to be written.

It has been three years since I discovered with absolute certainty my biological father is not my father. It has been two years since I learned the truth of my deceased biological father. It has been a decade-long journey of questioning family, friends, and acquaintances, and I have not even touched the "tip of the iceberg." Although many of the people I have approached have shown embarrassment, anger, or avoidance. I am unwilling to avoid the truth.

To those who have shown an immense amount of love, grace, and openness, I will be forever thankful. There is no harm in opening your arms and heart to a stranger. You may learn you are a great deal alike and even find you could love them just as if they had always been in your life. In reading this story, I hope you can look at these Not-Parent Expected situations in an entirely different light, and you learn from the experiences and stories shared in this book.

In 2020, during the pandemic, I was finally successful in obtaining tidbits of the truth surrounding my conception. It ripped my world wide open with answers concerning the confusion in the back of my mind that I could never quite put a finger on. It is impossible to explain in appropriate words the amazing feeling of peace I now have knowing that I am not crazy. The niggling at the back of my mind for the last fifty-nine years is REAL!

It would delight me if you joined me in learning more about those of us discovering our heritage and family through DNA testing such as 23andMe and Ancestry.com. Both testing programs have brought insights and assisted in finding the truth. Maybe you are an NPE and in reading this book you will know for certain you are not alone! We remain the same people in many ways upon learning this news, but it can also profoundly change lives forever with the mere act of spitting into a tube.

There are several topics addressed and explained to better equip the reader with NPE facts and societal dynamics playing a part in every facet of our lives. The chapters are intwined with true stories from NPEs, my discoveries and experiences as an NPE, issues facing everyone in day-to-day interactions with some poetry and advice thrown in for a little icing on the cake. You will also find some humor thrown in, too. This is a heavy topic, so some levity was definitely needed.

ACT I

CHAPTER 1

If You Only Knew

I have and continue to learn so much about myself, family, friends, human nature, and the true kindness and cruelty of people through the discovery of my biological family.

So, you may be asking, Lezlee, how did you get to this point? What made you first start thinking something wasn't right? The answer is not an easy one, because the feeling evolved over time. Looking back, I am sure I started realizing there was something odd underlying my existence at a very young age.

My parents married after my mother graduated from high school in 1958 and they had my brother in 1961. They divorced, remarried (not sure of the date), had me in 1963, and quickly divorced again within six months of my birth. As I look back this was a tickle in the back of my mind, and I always wondered, "Why? What would make two people marry, divorce, Repeat?"

My father married my stepmother when I was three. My mother married my stepfather close to the same time. My stepfather raised me as his own. I had two truly amazing men in my life. Honestly, I just thought it was normal and the way things were supposed to be.

There were rifts between my mother and father through the years. Sometimes it was about custody and visitation, and other times it was about child support payments. I find it a little ironic my mother was fighting a man for child support when she fully knew I was not his child.

The first, big indicator there was an underlying secret came when I was twenty-six years old. It was my father's birthday, and I was taking him to El Chico to celebrate. I was recently married, but my husband was unable to go to dinner with us. We had a lovely meal, just my father and me.

As we were finishing our meal, my father made a comment about how much I look like my mother. Well, that was a no-brainer because everyone knows I am the spitting image of her. He didn't stop there and expressed how hard it was for him to be around me because I reminded him of so much of her. Wow! What was I supposed to say to that? I answered feebly, "Well, I can't really do anything about how I look and who I look like."

He said, "Well, if you only knew," and that was it!

No explanation.

No answer to my question, "What do you mean by that?"

An 800-pound gorilla was placed in my lap that would breed a lifetime of secrecy and no answers for three decades.

I went home, got in the tub, and cried my heart out. "If you only knew" became a phrase I would hear over and over and these words would have a powerful impact on me forever. They would become four little words I resented, but they also drove me to seek the truth.

Through my tears I shared this story with my mother, and she acted appalled he would say such a thing. And thus, the story began.

The Story

It is a knowing LOOK

a LOOK that can unlock your deepest FEAR

FEAR of Rejection

REJECTION that can strike you deep in your HEART

a HEART that is full of love but restricted by LIES

LIES that are much much more painful than the TRUTH

a TRUTH that could have set so many people FREE

FREEDOM from running, freedom from SECRETS

SECRETS that never should have been kept in the first PLACE

a PLACE of belonging and a need to be heard that most people never endure nor UNDERSTAND

UNDERSTANDING you did not make the decision to be betrayed or DECEIVED

DECEPTION that is a churning and underlying CURRENT

a CURRENT pulling you under until you can barely BREATHE

BREATHE in and out to push down the hurt, anxiety, and YES-the EXCITEMENT

EXCITEMENT to meet the family you never knew EXISTED

an EXISTANCE completely different in the past than it will be in the FUTURE

a FUTURE full of opportunity, discovery, an understanding of YOU

YOU-the true person that matters in the END

CHAPTER 2

Moment of Truth

You may be down the road of discovery, just beginning or wanting to get started.

My first dive into my genealogy was through Ancestry.com. Like many people who stumble upon these unknowns, several family members took the DNA test one Christmas for the fun of it. My mom, brother, husband, niece, and I all took the test at the same time.

Laughingly, we all teased my husband he was going to turn up British and not full blood Swedish (he is from Stockholm) because he looks just like Paul McCartney. I used to tease my sweet mother-in-law about having a fling with Paul back in the day. Of course, it added more fun to the story when we learned she had been in London at the time The Beatles were there in concert.

Everywhere we go, especially when traveling abroad, people constantly stop us and ask Magnus, "Hey, has anyone ever told you that you look just like Paul McCartney?"

We emphatically shake our heads, yes!

Little did we know it was going to be my DNA test that came up suspect. The vague feeling at the back of my mind would subside and dissipate at times. These tests brought it back to the forefront of my mind for a brief minute. However, I had no clue what I was viewing. At the time I was running a business and did not have the luxury to focus on the results. The discrepancies did not even trigger questioning the paternal side of my family with purpose.

We all just thought it was weird my results came up as 28 percent Scandinavian. Because when we looked at mom's results, there was NO Scandinavian, and my brother was in the 90 percentiles of being Great British. My results had very little correlation with my brother's results and varied greatly even from my mother. Since these initial tests I have learned this can be common and the more people taking the test the more the algorithms adjust.

The question of course was, "Where did that come from?" Mom just blew it off with comments about how unreliable these tests must be and there was no way I had that much Scandinavian heritage or she would lean in and say it must be coming from her side of the family, the Andersons. Good try Mom!

In telling the story of my DNA surprise the same questions prevail: "Did your mom actually know?"

"Was your mom nervous the truth was going to come out?"

Truly, I have no answer to these questions. She was the master at avoidance and, as you will learn later, "Gaslighting." I would ask her the questions and she would begin denying and accusing others of making up stories. She made me feel as if I was crazy and bringing ideas to life that did not exist. Now that I know the truth, the deception a hard pill to swallow.

During this process, we had lots of fun with a few surprises, but nothing showed definitively that my brother and I were half-siblings. My niece identified and brought up the fact there was something odd between the two of us. I was showing as a cousin once removed and not her aunt. Still, I was clueless as to what this all meant. At the time a cM* number had absolutely no relevance and you might as well have been speaking a foreign language to me.

---

* cM=Centimorgan=In genetics, a centimorgan or map unit which measures genetic linkage. The higher the shared cM the stronger the relationship between those two people.

It all went ignored until a few years later when my brother encouraged me to utilize 23andMe. There is nothing like opening your results and family tree with a resounding "half-sibling" staring you in the face. The landscape of emotions is impossible to describe. I was shocked but also felt immensely free knowing I had not been chasing unicorns. This was real life statistical proof.

I am proud of my brother for encouraging me and for his reaction: "You are my sister and always will be. This changes nothing!"

Thank God for the kindest words he could have spoken to me in that Moment of Truth!

DID YOU ASK?

I ASKED......

Why are people saying what they are saying?

Why are they acting weird around me?

...AGAIN

Where are people getting this information?

Why are they saying they were never allowed to meet me?

What does my Dad mean when he says, "If you only knew"?

...Again Ten Years Later

Why would my DNA test not match my brothers?

Why do I not have the same results as you?

...One More Time

Is there a Possibility?

Could there be another option?

What are you hiding?

......Over and Over

Believe me I Asked!

PEOPLE THAT LOVED ME ASKED...

Are you OK?

What can I do to help you?

Why would they not tell you the truth?

Did you ask your mom? Did you ask your dad?

How did you find out?

PEOPLE WITHOUT A CLUE ASKED...

What is your Goal?

Why do you need to Know?

Why can't You just leave it Alone?

Why would you want to disrupt other people's lives?

Why does it matter?

Questions are asked that often have no answers, nor do they deserve a reply.

And then there are those questions that need, crave, and beg for a response.

The answers can relieve, create, or prolong pain.

They are answers we may not want to hear.

Don't let that stop you.

Just ASK and prepare to listen.

CHAPTER 3

A Funeral, a Surprise & a Baby (Baby Lezlee, that is)

An immense amount of time passed before the differences in the Ancestry DNA results would cross my mind again and when my brother encouraged me to take the 23andMe test. It was one of those "out of sight, out of mind" things. So, if it seems like there is a gap in time, well there is a huge gap: seventeen years, to be precise.

Around 2006, my stepmother was diagnosed with Lou Gehrig's Disease (ALS). The two of us did not have a tumultuous relationship. It would be fair to say we just never had much of a relationship at all. She was never demonstrative with me, nor had she ever told me she loved me.

As I child, I remember feeling like she really did not like me much. Being a people pleaser from a young age made this very hard to accept. I think it was the beginning of my amazing ability to walk away from painful situations with others. Walk away first before they hurt you. It is called sabotaging, and I became a master at it. It has taken many years of counseling to overcome. I can remember thinking I had a mom, so why did I care? However, looking back, I regret not trying harder to have more interaction with my stepmother. I am a person who does not believe in living with regrets, so this is a powerful statement about the past.

The most tender moment with her occurred during a visit to the hospital in her final stages. As I left that day, knowing it would be the last time I would see her, I turned to say goodbye. Since she could not speak, the only thing she could do was sign language and she signed "I love you."

I absolutely fell apart when I got to my car. Writing this after more than a decade still makes me cry. It shows how important and impactful it is to tell others how you feel and that you love them, especially children. Her simple and final gesture is embedded into my memory forever.

Sadly, she passed a few days after my visit. The transformative scene that plays over and over in my head was at my stepmother's funeral. My husband and I traveled to Van Alstyne, Texas for the service. We were mixing and mingling, holding Dad's hand to keep him calm and doing the things you do at a funeral. Nature called, and returning from the bathroom, a woman, a total stranger, approached me and exclaimed, "Baby Lezlee! You are Baby Lezlee, right?"

Needless to say, I was speechless and tried to explain that I was Lezlee, but I was confused as to why she was calling me Baby Lezlee.

She introduced herself as one of my stepmother's three sisters and they had all wanted to meet me my entire life but had never been allowed to do so. Yikes! What was this woman talking about? I had never heard their names nor been aware of their existence. Caught off guard and extremely uncomfortable, I tapped danced around a question for which I had no answer and left the funeral with many unknowns. How was I to respond?

Back home the following week I met mom for a glass of wine at our favorite place, The Keg. Introducing the topic was not difficult because I was clueless about any underlying issues and was totally innocent. This was the beginning of the gaslighting by my mother, and I would endure this behavior for years to come.

When asked she responded with, "Oh that is not true! They never asked to meet you." Ouch!

Here was a stranger telling me she and her sisters had wanted to meet me and my mother was telling me they did not want me, and this woman was lying to me. Here is the problem with lying to someone with tenacity: we never give up. There are people who, when confronted with fibs and convoluted stories, begin to become curious. Mystery solvers of the world rarely let it go. I happen to be one of those people. By the age of forty-eight, you would have thought my mother would have recognized this in my character. The more she avoided it and led me in different directions, the more I dug in to flush out the lies and get to the truth.

Being raised to never lie, this did not set well with me, but in my naivety and love for my mother, I believed her. Why would my own mother and dearest friend keep the truth for me?

The Gaslighting was Heating Up.

CHAPTER 4

Gaslighting-Girl on Fire

Before going any further, it is only fair to explain gaslighting. Gaslighting is a form of psychological abuse in which a person, sometimes a group, causes another person to question their sanity, perceptions of reality, and memories. When a person is being "lit" it can cause confusion, anxiety, and feelings that they cannot trust themselves. The term originally comes from a play in 1938 and a 1944 film titled *Gaslight*. In this drama, the husband manipulates the wife into thinking she has a mental illness.

Gaslighting can present itself in many forms. Though it is often witnessed in domestic abuse and violence, it can also rear its ugly little head in other situations.

Here are a few examples:

1. DENIAL—A person refuses to take responsibility for their actions. He or she may pretend to forget the past or a circumstance that occurred. The person will commonly blame someone else for their behavior.

2. WITHHOLDING—This is when people pretend they do not understand the conversation or the question. They might even refuse to listen or act as if the person talking is confusing them. "I don't know what you are talking about."

3. TRIVIALIZING—The person acts as though the concern is not important or makes one wonder why they are "making such a big deal of everything."

4. DIVERTING—Changing the focus of the discussion. Making the other person feel guilty for asking. The focus of the comments and questioning is shifted off of them back to the person questioning.

"That is ridiculous."
"I don't know what they are talking about."
"I wasn't a slut." (More on that later)

People experiencing this behavior can find it difficult to recognize the signs. They often trust the person that is acting this way. It can make the receiver feel unsure and second guess themselves.

This can especially occur when they have no memories of what the truth actually is, and they are relying on others to assist them in getting to the answers. It can make them believe they are being irrational, crazy, and defensive, thus causing them to constantly apologize for bringing up a topic or asking pertinent questions.

The tactic is often used to manipulate and isolate a partner or family member, undermining their confidence in a situation, and making them easier to control. I am sure it feels differently for everyone, but for me it made me mad. Mad in two ways: crazy mad and angry mad! Was I imagining all of this? No, that was impossible because this information was coming from others, not just from my imagination. This was real. I was sane. And someone was lying. Now came the angry mad. Catching people in more and more lies and gathering bits of the truth begins to grind on the heart and mind. In turn, it can create bitterness if we allow it. To survive, I retreated to humor. (Later I learned my biological father had a quick wit, was very funny and was always into something as a child: characteristics

I am proud to share with him.) This can come across as being flippant and uncaring. In reality, it is just a way to deal with a difficult situation without it eating you alive. There is no right or wrong way to handle these DNA/NPE situations, but it is important to find a way to keep your perspective and positive attitude or it can create some mental health issues.

Gaslighting has been around for years, just like ghosting, but it is finally coming to the forefront as abusive behavior and has been given a name. An article titled "What is Gaslighting" by Jenner Huizen appeared in *Medical News Today* in 2022 and is a terrific reference explaining the anomaly. I highly recommend reading this article if you feel this is happening to you or if you desire to learn more.

Abyss

There is a hole in her heart that will not go away
She tries to fill it with living things every day
But it empties again and again
She works
She prays
And some days hides from it all
Wishing for the emptiness to diminish
It is persistent
        Unavoidable
          And elusive
At times it is painful
At times it subsides and is bearable but
It is a deep and dark abyss that cannot be filled
Hugs
Kisses
Kind Words
        Cannot quench its hunger
It is like a grave that has not yet received its occupant
        Barren
        Cold
        Unyielding
Food, Friends, Frivolity
Help for a while and yet there it is,
        Emptiness-once again
And she realizes that only through God can she ever be whole
        So, she prays some more and slowly
        Ever so slowly
She can feel the edges of her heart begin to mend.

CHAPTER 5

Knock Me Over with a Feather— Lorna's Story

There are so many wonderful people I have met over the past few years. People in pain. Some fight, kick and scream through the discovery while others ease through it all with absolute solitude and an "it is what it is" strategy. It is worth repeating over and over that there is no right or wrong way to feel. There are good, better and best ways to approach others, but feelings are feelings, and we must own them or we will never get to the healing that is necessary.

Meeting people going through the same struggle is the beautiful part of the NPE world. Some chose to not speak about their outcome, and some, like me, desire to share it all. For many it is the first steps to healing, and others want no part of the connections. Being a part of a community was vital for me and I continue to pursue friendships and relationships with those that are on the same trajectory. Lorna and I met at a NPE retreat and have remained in contact ever since. It will be a lifelong bond. She was kind enough to share her story and this is merely one excerpt of her writings. I chose it because it engages the feelings and sense of panic, fear and shock that can happen when a DNA Surprise occurs. It can leave a person grasping for an explanation.

Here is her story in her own words:

It was an average day. I had begun to back out of day-to-day work and was semi-retired. We had sent off our samples of saliva several weeks before. Darrell's results (my husband) came back first and were a mix of everything. My results took a little longer, but finally they popped up in my email. There are no warnings or disclaimers or disclosures before you open this information—or there weren't any signals then. So, when I opened the email up, I was shocked to see almost 50 percent Greek in my report. My first thought was, though my mother's maiden name was McFadden, there had to be some mixture there. She also had dark hair, and I was supposed to look like her side of the family. So, shocked, yes, concerned, no. I called my sister, Devon, in to the office (she works for us) and asked her if she would care to do her DNA. She readily agreed. Meanwhile, my husband was looking at me and saying, "You know what this means, right?"

And I was saying, "It means nothing! I can explain it! You will see once we get my sister's results!"

Denial ain't just a river in Egypt! A few weeks later, her results came back. Devon had NO Greek heritage. Now, I was starting to panic, but still trying to make sense of it.

I went to my eighty-year-old mother and told her I needed her DNA. She looked at me and asked why. I exclaimed, in a somewhat exacerbated tone, "Because I'm GREEK! And Devon isn't! And I need to know what is going on!"

Why she didn't just confess then, I do not know, but she agreed to do the test, begrudgingly. She asked me, "What if it comes back that I am not Greek?"

I said, "Well, Mom, then we need to talk."

She never said a word. A few weeks later, her results came back and as expected, she has no Greek DNA in her profile. By this time, I knew in my heart, but my head was still trying to find a way around the fact that my dad was not my birthfather. I went to my mom immediately and her words were poignant. "Maybe, I have blocked it all."

She was not going to give this burden she had carried for sixty years up easily. I told her I loved her and that it didn't matter. I deserved to know the truth; for medical reasons, if no other.

I explained I wasn't mad or upset, but I was going to find the truth whether she helped me or not. Every so often I would visit her, and state facts like, "I recently found out that in 1956 a six-month gestation baby would have weighed about two pounds and probably would not have survived. I weighed four-and-a-half pounds. Premature? Yes! That premature, no.

I had found no close DNA matches, but a lot of distant Greek cousins were popping up. I was desperately searching but hitting dead ends everywhere. One day, Darrell was boarding a flight to China for business, and I got a text from my mother. It said, "His name was something starting with a C or a K and ending in—is or—as. He was stationed at Parks Air Force Base in 1955. We met at a USO dance. I didn't sleep around with anyone else, so when I became pregnant, I knew it was his. Please don't be mad at me. I was trying to protect you. I had lost one child and I was determined to have you and love you."

I cannot describe the feeling I had at that moment. The closest I can come to explaining is that it felt like a black hole had opened under my feet and half of me was sucked into the black hole . . . gone forever.

Let me reiterate that Lorna's feelings and sense of the ground opening underneath is common. Describing this emotion and sense of loss can hopefully assist those on the outside looking in to better understand the desperation and overwhelming discord it creates. On the other hand, if you are the person hearing the news, be encouraged by the fact this is normal and human. Nothing is wrong with you: own your truth and decide on your course of action.

CHAPTER 6

Metaphorically Speaking

I adore music, cliches and metaphors. Why, you might ask? It is a simplistic answer: Music because the words touch my soul. Cliches make me laugh and, though trite, have some simple and old-fashioned reasoning. Metaphors use words and phrases to create an idea or teach a lesson. Music has always been a part of my life. Though I cannot sing a lick my great uncle was a music writer, and his best-known song is "Silver Threads and Golden Needles." Listening to that song brings me great pride. It is an honor to be a part of such a legacy. Though many younger people may never have heard of this song, lots of people light up when they hear the title and are reminded of the tune. Though my singing abilities are not strong I can still "cut a rug" and dance with the best of them, with or without wine.

Cliches (or sayings) were a part of life growing up in Texas. Some of my favorites include:

"Don't throw the baby out with the bath water" (Look this one up, it is interesting)

"Well behaved women seldom make history."

"Be the Kind of Woman that when your Feet Hit the Ground in the morning Satan says, "Oh shit, she's awake."

Metaphors paint a picture as we tell a story. They lead the reader to interpretation. This interpretation is in the eye and the mind of the reader, and it helps us visualize various outcomes and options. The DNA discovery initiates the thoughts of many metaphors. The scenarios can play out like a scene from *Forrest Gump*: "*Life is like a box of chocolates. You never know what you are going to get.*"

This is true for everyone involved in the journey, so be prepared if you are involved in this pioneering world of discovery. NPEs are not the only ones having their life shifted, changed, and in many cases, turned upside down. This metaphor highlights how many things are completely out of our control. Some good things happen, and sometimes bad things happen. It is a mixed box, and we will never like every flavor. Personally, you can always leave out the creamy cherry-filled chocolates. It is one of the few foods that will never cross my lips and move onto my hips. Just like those icky cherry-filled candies, there are people on this journey that are, well, just icky, and I can leave them in the box.

If you are an NPE, a seeker of your truth or the truth of another, treat the journey with kindness. None of this is easy for the parties involved. Of course, there are times when it is pure joy and no one is being snarky, scared, or mean, but that is not true in many cases. There is usually someone in the picture who will be a catalyst for negativity. It is just life, and it is best to move on. Onward and upward as they say!

It was confusing and hurtful in the beginning when I was treated poorly by my half-sisters and first cousins. Confusing, befuddled, and hurt are just a few words to describe how their reactions affected me. But through research and being involved in a couple of Facebook pages and organizations, it became very apparent this was not just about me! I know, I know, I was pretty selfish at the time, and I had to have a reality check and get my bearings. It was hard for me to believe someone did not particularly want me around or to take a chance in getting to know me. I do not consider myself a narcissist, in case anyone out there is trying to diagnose these thoughts and feelings. It was more about the excitement of *finally* finding out the truth. Why wouldn't everyone else be as excited as me about these newly-found answers and truth?

WOW!

What an "aha" moment as Oprah would say.

Stepping back and analyzing my position was paramount if I was going to survive. Thus, the next metaphor that began to come to fruition in my mind. This discovery had been "marinating." Like a chef marinates meat to prepare for a delicious meal I had been steeping, soaking, and absorbing the seasonings doused on me for years. Just like meat when it has been marinating too long it can become dry, mushy, or tough. I had been preparing for the truth. Twenty plus years of marinating in the comments and secrets, learning the truth one step at a time made me tough and even possibly insensitive because of the lies and deception. I was not going to be the "victim" any longer. That was exactly how I felt, and when the truth did expose itself, I was hurt, angry, and dry to other people's potential feelings. Then I became mushy, and the tears would just flow. There are days I can be sharing this DNA journey and tears stream steadily down my cheeks. No rhyme or reason. It just happens.

Marinating Moment: The beginning of the story provided the seasonings but there were scenes that played out over the years that stirred moments of bafflement. These moments happened over time, a long period of time, which kept a slow burn to my questions and confusion. Family and strangers alike poured fuel onto the fire. At times they did it innocently and at times they did it down-right cruelly.

Many NPEs share these same experiences and wonder what is going on and drown in feelings of being lost. Questioning ourselves and others becomes a part of our daily life. Maybe we don't carry the turmoil every day, but incidents happen that bring it to the forefront again.

Words of Wisdom from this chapter

Trust Your Gut: Trusting your gut means following your intuition. Intuition is the little voice in your head telling you what's right and wrong. It's the thing that makes you feel like something isn't right, even if you can't explain why. Trusting your gut means listening to the voice and acting on it. I knew something wasn't right, but my "trust" lay with my love and dedication to my mother. What many people will say is, "She did it for you." or "Maybe she didn't know who the actual father was." Or my favorite, "Maybe she lived the lie for so long she began to believe it."

These thoughts and sentiments are probably accurate for those keeping the secrets.

However, true or not, it does not remove the feeling of betrayal. The opportunities for someone to explain usually occurs time after time with no yielded results. I asked the right questions, but the answers were not forthcoming. My gut knew there was more to the truth, and I was not going to give up. So, I marched forward and continued to seek and work on the necessary personal growth.

Healing through music and meditation is a good start to get a handle on our emotions, no matter what piece of the jigsaw puzzle you hold. The seeker, supporter and adversary all play a huge part in this game of truth and honesty. Each move on the proverbial chess board positions you or your opponent for the next action. Will it be stalemate or checkmate? The outcome has numerous potential directions, but in the end we each must own our individual truth.

Need a little inspiration through the day? Melody Beattie is part of my daily devotional time and has helped me immensely to keep balanced and structured with my new findings. If you buy her book, be sure to read the excerpt on page 21 for January 21. *Discover Your Own Truth*. It is very thought provoking.

The Truth Seekers

All we yearn for is to know our past.

We really don't think that is too much to ask.

You push us away as though we want something like wealth and money.

If the thought of that were not so cruel it might be funny.

As we travel down this desolate highway The Truth is all we Seek.

Yet, you have made the decision to run from the facts of which we will never speak.

You hold the power and control

of the beginning we will never know

Our journey continues day after day, night after night with no answers.

If only you would be so kind to relieve our questions

we could cut the strings of our mental dancers.

They Tango, and Waltz,

They Twirl and Spin

All the while our only desire is for you to stop the insanity and provide us an End.

CHAPTER 7

My Cousin Melody

Mud cakes in the driveway, Grandmother Ballard's amazing cooking, Saturday Night Wrestling, Christmas Eve, Antiques, Creativity. These are just a few memories that take me back in time and remind me of my cousin Melody. When we were young, she was more like a sister. Time creeps up on us and people go their different ways. She was raising children and I was building a career and managing businesses. Life just got in the way, and we spent less and less time together.

As her kids grew up and business relaxed, we caught up with one another more and more as we moved into our fifties. If anyone would know there was something up with family and this gut instinct of something being off, she would know it. Just to give you a lay of the land, Melody is my first cousin. Our fathers are brothers, and we spent most of our youth together.

Meeting her one afternoon for a glass of wine and some sunshine by the pool I popped the question, and she dropped the bombshell.

Me: Hey, have you ever known that I might not be my dad's child?

Her: Oh absolutely! Your dad is Tommy Candrell.

Me: What the Hell?! That is not possible. That was mom's best friend's husband!

Her: I know. It is crazy.

Me: Where did you hear this?

Her: From my dad.

Me: And you never told me? Why?

Her: I don't really know. I guess I thought you knew. Why do you think you were always kept away from dating the Candrell boys? I just thought you had figured out they were your half-brothers.

ME: Seriously?

HER: Or maybe I was afraid it might hurt you?

Me: OMG! Pass the wine!

No 'freaking out' allowed! Well, you can if you want.

Something very common in this DNA World of Surprises is that many people may know the truth about your heritage, but they assume:

1. You already know

2. They don't want to be the person that brings the truth to light

3. *Awkward*

This elephant (or 800-pound gorilla) is being eaten one big friggin' bite at a time.

I am hungry for more, but at times I am stuffed to the gills with new information and directions to turn.

Chew, chew, digest.

Research, research, marinate.

One more step toward the truth-tears and a bit of indigestion.

What am I facing?

My uncle is not my uncle (but he really is because I grew up with him)
My cousin is not my cousin (wait, you can't change that relationship).
My dad is not my dad (well, dog doodie).

These people are still my peeps, and no one can take that away.
Nor will I ever turn from them. They are my family and always will
be, but things got a lot more interesting.

We will see anything we want when we are searching for the truth.
At least I was seeing an opening at every turn. The imagination goes
wild. Blindly, following every lead. Praying for an answer. Hoping
for a resolution to the confusion.

Your mind races with the "what ifs" and a million scenarios begin
to formulate in the brain. These thoughts want to make an entrance
and the primary goal becomes getting to the bottom of the mystery.
Some of my mind swirling included unexplainable and complicated
outcomes:

- Friends and family kept me away from the Candrell boys
  because we must be related.

- They must have known.

- I spent time with Elsie Candrell, their grandmother.

    She must have been my grandmother, too.
    That is why I spent time with her.

- I kind of look like her.

- Wasn't she Swedish? That explains the Scandinavian. Oh wait,
  Mom says she is German. Do I believe Mom any longer?

- I had a huge crush on Kacey Candrell. That is why he could
  never like me, because he was my cousin or my brother. (Truth:
  He just didn't like me, and I really was not that cute.)

- There is this whole big family out there and I have been around them my entire life.

- They already know me and love me.

    This is it. I feel it in my bones. Finally, the answer. Oh boy, reel yourself in sister. Que the needle of the record player screeching across the record.

CHAPTER 8

Melody's Love Letter to Me

After our talk and the revelational information, I requested Melody to write what she remembered about our childhood and our relationship. The following is what I consider her love letter to me. If it sounds like it is not in my words, then it makes perfect sense because these are purely her thoughts.

> *Lezlee, don't laugh too hard as my sixty-one-year-old brain tries to reconcile childhood memories with heartfelt love. As you are aware our views change with lenses of age, experience, and time.*
>
> *When you were first journeying into your "new-found" truth it was a mystery to be solved and worthy of Jessica Fletcher herself! Just like Jessica or better yet, Nancy Drew, you dug in and went searching. The craziest thing to me is while we were searching for clues, drawing conclusions, and deciphering fact from fiction the truth was being kept under lock and key. The reason for hiding your past was out of love, I'm sure. Life in the sixties and seventies was definitely different than it is today. Not much is buried or behind closed doors in our current time like it was in the past.*
>
> *I was so happy for you when the veil of secrecy was drawn back, and your past came into better focus. Your realizing that you were not crazy about the confusing vibes was probably so freeing. I also*

felt and feared a loneliness I cannot explain. I am so glad the past we lived is a Fact! The days of love, adventures, and dreams shared were real. No amount of "new truth" can change or diminish our past and future together. I love you for you and our relationship beyond measure.

I recall us sitting back, sipping wine, and listening to you unravel your DNA story for me. You were thinking out loud about the what, why, and above all else, the who? The intrusive memory of my dad disclosing his thoughts about your birth enveloped me. Instantly, I was transported back to the curb of Nanny's house as he shared with me his version of the story. I knew then I had a clue (drunken as it might have been) and it might help you. We were mulling over the idea that you might have been related to the Candrell family.

We talked about how, if this were true, it made sense you were kept away from the Candrell boys, and it made total sense to the two of us in the moment. It is astonishing how small beliefs snowball and take on a life all their own. Those assumptions can affect everyone and everything in its path. As in Holmes and Watson tradition, we continued to contemplate the possibilities and where the facts might lead us. You began to formulate a plan to tackle the truth-seeking mission before you.

Our childhood created a relationship most would envy. We were cousins, friends and inseparable, just like sisters! Being with your family meant I was allowed to be a kid and have company. I wasn't ever by myself when I was young, and then I was with you and finally got to be "by myself and without my baby brother." Adventures, creativity, sleepovers, playing outside, unbridled imagination, and FUN were all a part of your household! Many of the things I considered then and still today was "outside the norm" for most kids. Your mom exposed us to creativity with trips to the Quadrangle, Sample House, and even to Canton First Monday in the ice and snow one January.

Favorite food treats also came with those trips specific to the places we visited. The atmosphere of your home always reflecting whatever art your mom was creating at the time: weaving, furniture making, basket weaving, Southwestern decor, beadwork, jewelry, dried flowers and herbs, and even raising chinchillas. Aunt Joan included all of us. We built forts, climbed trees, had Chinaberry fights, made mud pies, created our own language (somewhat like Pig Latin), and got your brother, Todd, in trouble whenever we could.

My memories of us were always at our grandparents or at your dad and stepmom's house. My memories are very faded when it comes to us being together at my house or my mom's antique store—odd isn't it? I know we spent a lot of time there, but I seem to have blocked it out.

As we grew older our visits lessened, but each time we are together it is like no time has passed at all. We have always been able to keep up through the grapevine and I still feel close to you even though it is has been a long time since our last get together.

My Lezlee (your nickname will always be Bo to me)

First and Foremost: You are independent. You have had that going for you "Forever!" I see the passion and love you pour into all you take on. People, projects, business…Life. You have taken what I would consider "dreams" and turned them into reality. Your artwork, cookbook, writing, radio show, and businesses have all been successful and you go after everything with gusto. My entire life has been about pleasing others and supporting them to chase their rainbows. As I have grown older, these traits of yours, that may have been considered selfish when I was young, I now applaud as fortitude and courage to live your life and make your dreams a reality.

I see your passion in all you do, and you live it with your entire being. Your wardrobe, vivaciousness, and above all your sassiness are amazing and special. As your loved one, I have witnessed the depth of your sadness, frustrations, confusion, and disappointment surrounding your DNA surprise, but, in all this, the main I see is your ability to overcome, ride the waves and, rise above the pain.

Keep on Keeping on Girl!

Love you with all of my heart,

Melody

This letter took my breath away, and no matter how many times I read it there are waterworks. This woman has always been an essential part of my life and when I asked her to share her feelings and thoughts this is the love she so eloquently expressed. If you are helping someone on their NPE path this is a great example of how words and compassion can ease the pain.

If we could all learn to be so kind and heartfelt what a better place this world would be. I love you my cousin, friend, and sister in life. The hope from sharing this letter is to instill the understanding that no matter how rough the waves might be there is someone who feels this way about you. Seek them out and let them know you think the same way about them, for these are the angels you need in your corner as you navigate the next turns.

CHAPTER 9

The Truth Teller—
I Can't Make This Stuff Up!

There are times when this trek has been absolutely hilarious. Finding the humor in tough moments can be considered ill-mannered or flippant, but for some laughter is the only medicine to get through the battle and end victorious. In asking questions and stories shared by a few new family members I have learned my biological father and grandmother were both extremely quick-witted, always making people laugh and real cutups.

My mother was also very funny. Not a knee-slapping, jokester but she was a bit mischievous and astonishingly private. She was humorous in a way that her antics could induce eye-rolling, "I can't believe she said that," or "She did not just say that," kind of amusing. She always had an ear to listen and a shoulder to cry on or lean on, whichever was the case. I share this because people get confused by my telling this story and think I am dissing her in some way. That is the furthest thing from the truth. In fact, the reason the story is being told is because she was never able to tell it herself. Shame and fear of judgment kept her silent.

Being raised in a staunch Southern Baptist household gave her little to no options other than being private and secretive. Now I get to be her voice and let it be known that these things happen, and it is okay. We should not judge. In her generation, acceptance and forgiveness was a rarity, not a commodity as it is today. Society today forgives transgressions no matter what the cost and the damage to others.

Enough of that. Back to the funny stuff.

Remember I had a name in my back pocket given to me by Melody, and I was ready to fire it at mom when the time was right, and when she least expected. This had become my modus operandi. If I gave her too much time to think, she figured out how to avoid the topic at hand.

TOPIC AT HAND: Who's My Daddy?

I never said I was right about how I handled each step or encounter. Nor do I give any illusion the best tactics were utilized, but at that point it was all about strategy. None of us know how we will deal with this until we are there. Even then, there is no guidebook on how to act. In theory however, it is a great idea to produce such a manual.

The opportunity presented itself soon after my eye-opening encounter with my cousin. Mom and I are sitting in front of the bank manager adding me as Power of Attorney and signatory on mom's accounts. It was pretty busy and loud in the bank, and we were wrapping things up. I took my moment:

Me: Hey, so Mom, I was with Melody yesterday and I asked her about the possibility of Bill not being my dad.

Mom: Oh really? What did she have to say?

Me: That I am correct about Bill not being my Father and that Tommy Candrell is my dad.

Mom: What? Are you sure she didn't say Sonny Candrell? (Tommy's Brother)

Me: (Speechless for a moment and jaw dropped) Well, is that an option?

Mom: Well, more so than Tommy!

Banker: (With eyes diverted, looking down, and sweat on her upper lip) Oh my—well, ladies I think we are all good and wrapped up here.

Me: Whoa, whoa wait a minute! You have got to be kidding me, Mom! You are killing me, Smalls.

At this point I was numb to the gaslighting and recognize her avoidance tactics, so I chose to laugh and stay calm. Getting all wonky wouldn't do anyone any good, especially the poor bank manager sitting in on the conversation. Breathe in and out, repeat. "Okay, well, let's go get that glass of wine at Macs," I said.

You may notice that lots of my conversations end with a glass of wine. She had too much time to figure out how to evade the discussion once again during our drive in our different cars to the restaurant. My plan of attack for information was thwarted once again.

Step-by-step the story was unraveling and was beginning to eat at me because every morsel of information seemed to chip away at my resolve to figure it all out. The tears had not inundated me yet. I was only on the cusp of this adventure, and it percolated in my gut like soured milk, not sure if the pain would pass or if it would result in making me ill.

CHAPTER 10

Her Best Friend's Funeral

The bank incident passed and once again the darkness and lack of answers took hold. There was an open door, though, and I intended to step through it like it was a portal in a fantastical sci-fi movie.

By golly I've got it! I had a name to chase down, research and cultivate a plan of action. Boy, oh boy, was I going to get to the bottom of this, finally. Mom was back to gaslighting and there was no way I was stopping. At this stage, my determination might have needed a bit more discretion.

Learn from my mistakes and believe me when I say, "take it easy." Take it easy on yourself and on others. For instance, you may have had a long time to absorb different aspects of the situation, while others are hearing about it for the first time. Give them grace and time. I am not advocating giving up when you get "no" for answers. Just saying let other parties absorb while you continue your search.

You do have the right to the truth, but naivety about what is learned and what the future holds can far outweigh the excitement you can feel with each step forward. Those two steps forward can quickly evolve into ten steps back. Not a dance you want to choreograph.

Another turn of events came a few months later and it afforded me an opportunity to ask more questions. My mom's lifelong friend passed away on January 4, 2018. Never to be outdone, Mom followed her the same year in December, and as the saying goes "she took the secret to the grave."

If you recall from the last chapter, two names came into play, Tommy and Sonny Candrell. Tommy was my mom's lifelong friend's husband. Following all of this takes a little bit of effort to keep up, so any confusion is understandable. Her friend's funeral was lovely, and another dear friend hosted everyone for a Celebration of Life. Of course, my mom's friend's sons (my potential first cousins or half-brothers) would be there. Their names were Tommy, Jr. and Kacey. My mission, if I chose to accept it, was to delicately address the paternity topic with at least one of the boys to see what they said and how they reacted.

And before you go all, "Oh no Lezlee, you did not ask them if their father was your father at their mother's funeral?!" rest assured I did not do that and do not advise an insensitive move like that under any circumstance. On the other hand, it felt safe to bring up the option of it being their Uncle Sonny. This would mean we were first cousins and armed with this information I would be able to blow the locks off this treasure trove.

First, necessary fortification, a glass of wine. No, I am not an alcoholic even though unraveling all of this was enough to make a teetotaler start drinking or a saint to start cursing. Wine, deep breathing, bathroom break, kiss on the check from mom, hugs from all my mom's astounding friends, and I am ready for the big moment. It was so important to do this right. The question I was prepared to ask may give me an answer I was not ready for and could change my life forever.

Was I ready?

Damned Straight I was!

Tommy Jr. and I have always been close. Kacey and I were too but in an odd way I was less afraid to confront Tommy, Jr. Leaning against the railing of the deck on an amazingly beautiful and unusually warm January afternoon, sipping a beer, I casually addressed the issue at hand. (I was approaching a guy drinking a beer with an extremely delicate topic so, hey, I am playing the beer drinking role).

Me: Hey, there is rather a weird question I need to ask you.

Tommy Jr.: Oh yeah, what would that be?

Me: Well, I have had some suspicion that Bill might not be my dad.

Tommy Jr.: Oh really? What makes you consider that?

Me: Well, it is a long story how I got to this place. Mainly, though I brought it up with my cousin, Melody, a few weeks ago and she mentioned the name Candrell which totally shocked me.

Tommy Jr.: That doesn't surprise me because we have all known for a while that Bill was probably not your biological father.

You could have pushed me over with a feather, as Lorna would say, and I hope my mouth did not drop open as far as it felt like it did. What the Hell? Here was another childhood family friend sharing the exact same sentiment of people knowing about this, and I was completely oblivious. When it happens once, we consider it could possibly be a fluke, but now I was on verification number, oh, let's say four, to keep it a good even number.

It was a warm January afternoon and my body temperature feels like it suddenly dropped thirty degrees, and probably not for the reason you are thinking. My reaction was not surprise, fear, or anxiety, it was all out, fully loaded-HURT! It was beyond my comprehension to fathom so many people knew for certain or speculated my heritage was something other than believed.

The pain from the deceit, lies, and betrayal burned a hole in my psyche. I did not want to be hurt by this, feel this pain, or accept so many friends and family had decided not to share what they knew. Yes, this was a hard thing to address with another person and I totally get why these lifelong family/friends were not forthcoming. But, by golly, my mother, who raised me to be a God-fearing woman and to be honest, true, and to never, ever tell a lie could have been honest and prevented me from walking into these mazes mixed with misdirection and confusion. The entire time she had been beating me over the head with the "honesty, bible verses, and theology," she was keeping the biggest secret of all. My lineage, history, and background.

People say:

"She was protecting you."

"She lived the lie so long she thought it was true."

"She didn't want to hurt you."

Yada yada yada! I call bullshit. The one person she did not want to hurt was herself.

The bottom line was I had been lied to throughout my life and the lies were still coming. At that stage and for the next several years, I would alternate between pissed, passionate, desiring to dig deeper, questioning myself if I was right or not, and hurt from not understanding why people hid behind this veil of deceit. Was there something wrong with me? Was I not trustworthy? Did they think so little of me they thought I would be angry at them or walk away forever?

None of these are traits I bear, so this added another layer of hurt onto the cake with a big ol'e pile of extra frosting. Unlike the cake with delicious layers and mouthwatering frosting, though this gave me absolutely no pleasure, at all.

The conversation continues:

Me: So glad everyone has known this little tidbit, except me. How did you know?

43

Tommy Jr.: Dad told Kacey and me many years ago that it was a possibility.

Me: Did your mom know?

Tommy Jr.: No, Dad told us that he had never mentioned it to her.

Me: Okay, I take some solitude in that. In bringing it up to mom she mentioned your Uncle Sonny's name. Is that who your dad thought it might be?

Tommy Jr.: Yes, that is who he thought it was.

Me: So, we could actually be first cousins and we never knew it. What should I do?

Tommy Jr.: Contact Uncle Sonny and tell him what you know so far. He is a good man and will help you any way he can. He would want to know.

For not being much of a beer drinker, two Bud Lights went down really fast.

A few days later I contacted Tommy Jr. to get his uncle's phone number. I was definitely going to adult this deal, so I called! We spoke briefly, and he wanted me to text him what I wanted to discuss.

Me: Uh, well, this is not exactly the kind of thing that would be appropriate to text you. It is a bit more serious than that.

Sonny: Okay, well then write me a letter and tell me what you think happened.

Okie Dokie, here we go.

ACT II

CHAPTER 11

Dear John Letter (Robert, Sonny or Don, whatever your name is)

Let me begin this chapter by saying anyone reading this book is welcome to utilize this letter as a template for correspondence you might want to create. Every letter will be different, but perhaps it will give you a foundation to build from as you begin your own letter. I have altered it slightly to not cause hurt or pain. Please excuse any possible editing issues because I am publishing this as close to the actual format as possible.

Dear Sonny,

I decided to sit down and write out the story of how I came to the point of contacting you. I am sure hearing from me was odd, to say the least. Yet, I did not want to go through the rest of life without reaching out and regretting I never asked or discovered the possible truth.

How did this all come about?

First, let me give you the names of the Characters in this story.

THE CHARACTERS:

1. Me-Lezlee Shontae Ballard (name on my birth certificate) Martin (stepfather's name but never adopted me) Liljenberg (married name). The passport division questions me a lot for all these names, and in between I married at the age of twenty-six and was "Haight" for a while.

2. Joan Reynolds Ballard Martin (my mother)

3. Bill Ballard (person I thought was my biological father)

4. Paul Martin (stepdad)

5. William Todd Ballard Martin (my brother)

Well, there are many more people involved but these are the main characters of the story.

And then of course, possibly:

You: Sonny Candrell

THE BEGINNING:

Joan married Bill right out of high school, and had my brother at the age of twenty. They divorced shortly after, and she was single and on her own. According to my calculations, Joan was probably single for about eighteen months before she and Bill remarried and I came along. Six months after I was born, they divorced again for good. I am aware she was still seeing him, along with other men, while she was single. So, when she found herself pregnant, it is assumed she convinced him I was his. Upon my birth, I think the "cat was out of the bag." I was almost "black" (probably more Spanish). I was dark with blue eyes. I had a full head of curly black hair.

You can get a laugh out of this: I was so dark that the black nurse took me back out of the room and checked the numbers to make sure I was in the right room. She told Joan, "This baby ain't yours!" It has always been a running joke in my family and told at my birthday every year. Little did I know. I think at that point Bill began to question and the truth came out, but they decided to cover it up. Lies are hard things to keep for so long but they did succeed until Bill's guilt and the belief I should know began to surface again. Why not just tell me?

Joan married Paul (stepdad) when I was three, and he raised me as his own for my entire life until he passed at the age of sixty-six and I was thirty. Bill was always in my life but at arm's length, in many ways. Of course, I always found the behavior odd. Guess I always thought it was because I had such a great stepdad he did not want to compete, but now I know there was more. It was hard on him and on many occasions I am sure he was not sure how to act.

THE QUESTIONS BEGIN

Fast forward to 1988/1989/1990: I was twenty-five and engaged to be married when Bill started making comments like, "If you only knew the entire story" or "You will just never know the truth." It brought me a lot of tears and heartache because no one would ever tell me what he was talking about. I went on with life, let it go and did not question it again. Why should I? I had a great family, they loved me, and I had the world by the tail! I have always believed there is enough love to go around, and blood is not all there is to our lives and loving (probably because I had such a great stepdad). Yet, here I am trying to find "my blood." Ironic, huh?

LIFE BRINGS MORE QUESTIONS

Around five years ago, my stepmother (Bill's wife), a person that never had much to do with my brother and I, passed away. We attended the funeral, and her sisters made numerous comments about how they had never been allowed to meet me and I was their "baby Lezlee" and "baby girl" they had never been allowed to know. It was a little weird, and I started asking questions again, totally unsure as to where all of this was coming from. Over time, I asked questions with no answers. Basically, I was told all of it was lies.

Little by little, I have broached the subject with both Joan and Bill. She began dropping some hints this was true, and then Bill began the old comments about "if you only knew the truth." Then he would shut up when I asked him to explain. At this point I was not going to stop, but I took my time. I stopped being so casual about it and dug a little harder.

ANCESTORY.COM STEPS IN:

Several years ago, I took the Ancestory.com test and my DNA came back 25% Scandanvian, 40% Great British, 21% Irish, 7% Iberian Peninsula, 5% Eastern Europe.

No big deal. But it did make me wonder because this was nothing like I had ever been told of my background. My brother finally sent in his own DNA. This was where we knew if something could be different this is where it would show up. My brother and I had completely opposite results. It was further proof we did not have the same parental make-up. He truly did not want to tell me, and I think he was more bothered by the discrepancy than me. I had already come to grips with the situation and have been fine with it all along. I think I have always known, so it came as no surprise, I find it to be a blessing. I also realize not everyone feels or thinks this way and I respect this as much as humanly possible.

THE NEXT STEP:

I approached my first cousin (or who I grew up thinking was my first cousin). I shared with her my discoveries, and she said, "Oh yeah, it is Tommy Candrell."

Of course, I said, "That is impossible; that's Mom's best friend's husband, and I grew up with all of them. There is no way!" We laughed, drank a glass of wine, talked about our crazy parents, and moved on.

But now I was unsettled. A few days later I was at the bank helping Joan with her financial issues. I dropped the bomb about being told my father was Tommy Candrell. Joan looked straight at me and said, "Tommy? Are you sure she did not say Sonny?"

So, I asked her if it were a possibility and she said, Well, way more than Tommy!"

Thus, your name was thrown into the ring, so to speak. Now, she completely denies it, is mad at me for continuing my search, does not understand my desire to complete this circle and wants nothing to do with my getting to the truth. Things kind of snowballed from there I am afraid.

THE END TO A BEGINNING:

The only people I knew left to ask were the boys (Kacey and Tommy Jr.). I grew up with them and always considered them to be like brothers. Life took us in different directions, but they were always a wonderful part of growing up. Tommy Jr. was on my "to call" list for months. I was too unsure of how to approach it. The main thing I have ever wanted was to just put my confusion to rest, never ever to disrupt anyone's life or to upset anyone. That is impossible to do without involving others.

I thank God for putting Tommy Jr. and me at the right place at the right time. I finally got the nerve to ask him and I knew he would shoot me straight. Now, whether he is right, or not, I don't know, but he shared the possibility of your being my dad had come up thirty years ago. He wondered what took me so long to start asking. WOW, I feel like everyone around me knew something and I was the last to know.

The timeframe of thirty years has come up often, and the only reason I can think it became a topic of conversation is because this is when I got married the first time. With my second marriage, I was older and no big ceremonial walking down the aisle stuff.

This is my journey and I recognize this may seem selfish in a way, but I promise you I have no ill intent nor want anything other than the facts. If I were to discover unknown family and they want me in their lives, it would only be a blessing. If not, I would understand. I still believe there is enough love to go around and the more people to love the better.

The other day at the celebration of Lydia's life I found myself looking at these wonderful people surrounding me. They may have been my family all along and I missed out on being around them and it made me sad. My only regret is I never knew, and I would have tried to be the best family member possible.

If you ever would just like to share the past it would be awesome. I always love hearing great stories. If it is something we could delve into further, then I would be thankful to share this journey with you later in our lives. This should only be in joy, never to bring discomfort or pain. I will take your lead and follow your wishes and those of your family. No hard feelings should this not be something you want to venture into further.

Sent to you in Love,

Lezlee

A few days after Sonny received the letter his wife sent me a text telling me she was happy I was looking for my biological family. She told me they would be happy to help in any way they could. This really boosted my spirits and dissipated some of the anxiety aroused in sending the letter.

Sadly, I must report they ghosted me immediately after this and never another word was received from them. It has been years, and Sonny's wife has passed at the time of publication. Admittedly, the silence hurt, especially when I witnessed a moment of interest and sincerity. It sparked hope.

What people need to grasp is the wake of destruction they leave behind when they throw the NPE a life preserver and yank it back just as quickly, leaving the NPE behind to drown or tread water. Either way, it is tiring and frustrating. None of us asks for this circumstance, so please recognize how your actions can cause great damage even though you may think it is not important. There is someone on the other end of the lifeline you just threw out, and they are depending on you to hopefully pull them to safety.

If you are unable to fulfill the offer of help, then it is highly recommended you never make promises you cannot keep nor give hope you are unwilling to provide. It makes the matter worse for all parties involved.

CHAPTER 12

Fifty Shades of DNA— Who's Your Daddy?

The title of this chapter went a million directions but after watching *The Book Club* (for the third time) it seemed like I was living a life of Fifty Shades of DNA. Shades of Grey had very little to do with the reason I used the title. Yet, it felt apropos because this journey seems to have no black and white but possesses a million shades of gray in every outcome.

In the movie *Fifty Shades of Grey* the title refers to the numerous facets of Christopher Grey's personality and is perfectly relatable for those seeking their past. There are so many aspects to consider and choices to be made upon learning one is an NPE.

Symbolically the phrase "shades of gray" usually refers to situations that are not often clear when the heroine or hero is dealing with potential evil. There is nothing cut and dry with how to behave or act after a discovery, thus another shade of gray appears.

Data has found that the human eye can see only thirty-two shades of gray. Experience suggests this DNA world may have more like 32,000 shades of gray on the spectrum. Every single one of us has a different story, various outcomes, and numerous results.

What's in a Name?

The other title in the running for this chapter was What's in a Name?

Come to find out-Everything!

By now you have the gist of how things were panning out with my search. Here I share the various names mentioned as options during long discussions and questioning Mom.

One of the first names mom supplied was Don Carter. If you are a bowling fan you are probably familiar with this icon, and many considered him as the sport's first superstar. Seemed like such a random name to throw out but the dates made sense even if he would have been thirteen years older than her. She always liked older men, so who was I to debate? This dude would have been right up her alley. When she first threw this name in the ring, I teasingly told her it was going to be very upsetting if all this time I had this wealthy father and she had kept me a secret.

Let me clarify that teasing Mother about the money was just a joke. Money is rarely ever the reason people are delving into their past. Too many shows, movies, and novels have created the misconception that everyone looking for family or the appearance of every illegitimate child is about seeking revenge or a wealthy family's inheritance. That is such hogwash, and this myth needs to be overturned and dispelled.

There was also Don Carter, the American investor and businessman, who was the founding owner of the Dallas Mavericks NBA team, and the Dallas Sidekicks soccer team. Over the years he owned many types of businesses, including a Rolls Royce dealership, banks, hotels, rodeo arenas, and ranches. Looking at the big picture this guy would have been considered a huge score in Mom's view.

Following instinct and gut reactions is a blessing and comes in handy if we will listen and follow their lead. In the case of both men, a stop-and-see tactic was best and proved, in retrospect, to be the correct strategy. She had me down two (Don Carter) rabbit holes, thus far, and then there was the third potential Don Carter.

DON CARTER THE ROCKABILLY

The story interceding here is the one about my great uncle, Dick Reynolds. As mentioned earlier, he was a songwriter and part of the Rockabilly movement in the 1940s. Rockabilly was an early form of rock music and originated with white performers in the American South. The music was literally rock and roll played by hillbillies, and Elvis Presley introduced the rhythm-driven music on his first recordings.

The history of the Rockabillies is fascinating and includes many names from the time that you might recognize. Names like Sonny Burgess, Buddy Holly, Marty Robbins, and Jack Rhodes, who co-wrote the song "Silver Threads and Golden Needles" with my uncle and Wanda Jackson, who cut a version of the same song.

This Don made more sense than any of the other Dons thus far. At the time this name presented itself, I was engaged in discussions with a gentleman in the United Kingdom who was writing a book about Jim Reeves. Mr. Reeves was part of the Rockabilly world, and my uncle was a part of that era.

This Don Carter co-wrote songs with Jim Reeves, Jack Rhodes, George Jones, and Darrell Felts. All names I recognized from my childhood. On a side note, the Rockabilly movement is rich in history. If you ever have time to check it out, go for it. You will not be disappointed. It is fascinating. Or visit The Texas Country Music Hall of Fame in Carthage.

The next transitional moment is scorched into my memory. Mom was in the hospital again. The name Don Carter was the last thing on my mind. Unbeknownst to me, there was not much time left on her life clock. Why would I think I was running out of time to unearth the truth?

As I entered the foyer of the hospital, my phone rang and it is my friend and author from the United Kingdom. In this particular and pivotal conversation, he briefly mentioned the name, Don Carter.

Me: Wait hold a minute, what did you say?

Friend: What? Don Carter?

Me: Yes, that name. Where did you get that name?

Friend: He is one of the Rockabillies and it is giving me fits trying to find information on him. I thought since he was in the timeframe and group with your uncle you might know something about him that could help unravel this mystery for me.

You could have heard a pen drop and I am pretty sure my heart skipped a few beats.

Me: No, I don't him, but I know someone who just might.

During the visit with mom, I briefly mentioned the name Don Carter but I did not want to get too deep into those waters yet. There was still research to do before that discussion could be initiated. Biting my tongue and biding my time was key at this point. Going in like a bull in a china shop was not the answer. First, I had to Google this man. Secondly, I and to determine if he existed and the potential timeframes. Third, see what he looked like.

This guy was elusive, and like my research friend said very little information was available. Nevertheless, my friend sent me a picture and I printed it for the next visit to the hospital.

There were no resemblances between the two of us but why would that matter? I looked identical to my mother and bore striking resemblances to most relatives on the maternal side of the gamut. This much was undeniable and not part of the puzzle so any man might or might not make sense.

Just like with the scene at the bank, I was prepared and ready to address the next encounter. I was off to the hospital, talking this through out loud during the drive.

How would she have met him? Well, there was the time she mentioned of hopping a train to Mineola and spending the weekend. If her dad had ever found out he would have killed her.

Was my Uncle Dick aware of this relationship? No big deal now. Both my uncle and Don Carter had passed away, so there was no one around to confirm or deny.

Could this guy make sense? The timing may have been off. Her meeting him may not have been feasible. It depended on when she made other trips to East Texas, and maybe she was part of the "jam session" or whatever they called it back then. Rockabilly hoedowns? For reals? I was all over the board and rightfully so. I needed and wanted answers.

Dead or Alive I wanted my man!

A little bit of background about how this Don Carter came to fruition as an option was shared with mom, and then I showed her the photo. Mom looked at it and asked:

Mom: Who is this?

Me: The man I have been telling you about and heard of from my friend in the UK who is researching Jim Reeves and the Rockabillies.

Mom: Hmmmm, I don't recognize him, but he sure was cute.

Me: Mom, is he a possibility?

Mom: Well, I wasn't a slut you know!

Me: Oy vey. Of course not, I never said that.

Mom: Well, you were much wilder than me. And you did much worse things than I did at that age. (Recognize the gaslighting here? Yep, full blown characteristics of gaslighting, so it is good to be able to identify this when it comes your way.)

Me: (My eyes widened, my heart raced). Well, yes, I am sure I did but this is not a competition. We are not playing tit for tat. I am just trying to piece together the players, and I use the word "players" literally and figuratively, Mom.

Mom: Well, I never did the stuff you did.

The answer is not going to be reveled this time either.

Laugh out Loud! Go ahead it is Okay! Yes, hand well played, mother, well played. The woman had been playing me like a good hand of Blackjack, and once again—Dealer Won!
I craved black and white. No Grey!
I lust for the truth.
Fifty Shades of DNA and way too many names were thrusting me into insanity.
If you only knew!
You're Damned straight! If I only knew anything I could have backed off half of the population, stopped probing into people's lives, and gotten some clarity.
Obviously, Joan and Bill were not going to provide me with that clarity any time soon. They had me jumping through hoops for sure. Some days I wonder how two people that never got along, constantly fought about my brother and me, and could barely manage an hour in the same room were absolutely steadfast in keeping one secret. This was no little secret. It was a fifty-eight-year-old confidence and commitment between the two that at least one of them was about to take to the grave.

Frank's Story

It is easy for some NPEs to share their story, and others fear they may hurt someone or experience retaliation if they go public. It is my privilege that these friends decided to offer pieces of their discoveries and what they encountered. It helps all of us to have a better understanding of the different scenarios that can possibly occur. Thank you to Frank for allowing me to share part of his journey. We all have a different voice and way we express ourselves, please enjoy Frank's candor. Here is his story:

> In 2012, after my wife had moved in with me but before we were married, we thought it would be fun to do one of those mail in DNA testing kits. My wife's results came back 99 percent Ashkenazi, at which she scoffed, because there was no way she would be anything less than 100 percent while my results were different than I expected. I had always been told I was half Catalan and half Polish, but the results indicated I was half Catalan and half Irish. I asked my mother about the results, and her response was that there was no possibility of anything strange or unknown. I believed her, thinking maybe they just hadn't worked out the errors in the lab.
>
> In 2017, I received a message through the DNA kit company from someone claiming to be my cousin. I asked my mom again, and she was emphatic that there was no possibility of anything strange. She suggested the sample was contaminated with someone else's in the lab, so I stopped asking.
>
> In April of 2022, my wife, and I were looking forward to the birth of our fourth child. We decided to look at some of the updated data on the website of the DNA kit company. We enjoyed theorizing about the eye color of our child, and decided to investigate the half-Irish situation. We signed up for a free trial with a census records website and spent the night using data to trace the relationship back

with someone listed as my second cousin once removed. We linked them to others, confirming we were on the right track. By morning, we had confirmed I was not related to the man I grew up thinking was my father, and we narrowed down my biological father and two of his brothers in Illinois.

Addressing my mother about it the next day, her entire demeanor changed. Gone was the constant reassurance I was the son of the man I grew up thinking was my father. In its place was the admission there had always been a doubt. The two of them had broken up briefly around the time I was conceived, while they were in college together.

She remembered attending several parties and slept with at least a couple of other men during that time. She remembered one of them and thought he could have been my biological father, but never pursued the possibility. She admitted she kept the truth of my origin for nearly forty years and asked me not to tell anyone. She was worried what her mother and brother would think. It was the moment I realized I could never again trust her, unconditionally.

The same day I contacted the brother of the man we learned had gone to the same college as my mother when I was conceived. He was shocked, having never had any idea I existed, but he was kind and open to speaking with me. I learned his mother passed away in 2014 and his other brother passed in 2019. This meant my mother's insistence the DNA kit result was wrong cost me the potential opportunity to meet my grandmother and an uncle.

Now, more than a year later, I have met my biological father and we have a great relationship.

He's made the trip to Maryland several times, spending time with my family, even having lunch with my mother. Neither of them remembers each other, so the best guess is they were under *the influence of substances and along with the passage of time, they are unable to remember the encounter.*

Frank's story is heartwarming and an outcome many NPEs would love to tell. Sadly, there were relatives he missed out on meeting because of denial and fear, but his story gives hope.

CHAPTER 13

Father's Day—Dad Comes Clean

There are many people who never know their father, thus never having a reason to celebrate Father's Day. In my youth it seemed like such a burden to have to celebrate two Father's Days. In retrospect, I wish that feeling of duty could have been replaced with true and pure enjoyment.

Don't get me wrong I loved my dads immensely. It just seemed awkward at times to make sure I honored both dads equally every year. It made it even more difficult when I rarely heard from one dad and then I had to be the one to make the effort on that special day.

Maybe I questioned why I was being ignored (or avoided) most of the time and not treated special. Yet, as a child, it was my duty to show up and be a good daughter. This is what I wanted every day of the year, but it was not happening.

Looking back almost all celebrations were a little like duality. Whether it was Christmas, Thanksgiving, or Easter my brother and I were pulled in two directions. This is a reality for many children, it is just a way of life. There are tons of fun things we can do to celebrate life with our fathers every June.

Have a picnic, go camping, finish a puzzle together, enjoy family game night, complete a task for your dad that he has been meaning to do, watch sports together, organize a BBQ, go bowling, attend a concert. The list is endless and looking back if I could rewind anything this is one area I would backtrack and change the results. I would have made Father's Day more adventurous and fun. Realizing how special these times could have been is a little sad and we all missed out in my opinion.

If you have the opportunity, rethink how you look at these chances to spend quality time with the men (or women) in your life. Hey, if I had known my biological father through the years, I would have had three men to celebrate. At this stage in life, it would have been a Godsend to have known all three of them.

So why am I going on about Father's Day? Well, about ten years ago Father's Days started getting tougher. Not because of the duality issue which by the way is defined as: an instance of opposition or contrast between two concepts or two aspects of something; a dualism. But the "If You Only Knew" comments became more common and created an atmosphere of dread.

My stepfather passed years ago, so Father's Day was a singular commemoration of my living male parent. It was enjoyable and breaking bread with my dad was a pleasure. It allowed us time to get to know each other better. However, little by little as he realized I knew the truth about my paternity things got awkward again. Each year he moved back into the old habit of saying,

"If you only knew."

"If you knew what your mother had done."

"You would not believe what your mother did."

Oh boy, here we go again!

Attempt followed attempt to get the answers and I was not above begging for him to spit it out. We were both reduced to tears on every occasion. Every Father's Day took on a new meaning, filled with anxiety, but I could not ignore him. He was and is my father.

Nothing could take that away, not even the Truth! He instigated the discussion each and every time, but, just like in the past, would leave without one more tidbit of information.

It drained me. Seriously, these kinds of conversations took every last ounce of energy. It would begin with nervousness for a week prior to the day and then escalate when the cards are on the table. Yet, in this case the dealer laid the cards but wouldn't play them. It was a cat-and-mouse game that had been going on for years, and it was exhausting.

Finally, enough was enough. June came around and I had committed to myself and to my husband I was not going to take the bait, nor would I bring it up. Mum was the word. Throughout all this, my poor husband watched the people he loves fall to pieces before his eyes. Afterwards, he watched me struggle again for weeks because I still had no answers. I was filled with frustration because I was being teased and tortured with the possibility of a name finally being revealed.

With 23andMe's confirmation of the discprency, my dad was aware of this. Rather than letting sleeping dogs lie, he approached the topic again. I thought I had made it to the finish line. Dinner had been wonderful, dessert tasty, and the wine delicious.

Ooops there it is! Pandora's box opened once again by the simple comment. "If you only knew."

At that point, those words became like a dagger to my heart. How could four simple words carry such a burden and strike such desperation? It was insane. Do you know the definition of insanity? Doing the same thing over and over and expecting a different result. Well, this time we needed a different result!

DAD: If you only knew

ME: Okay, Dad that is enough. If you know something, then just get it out.

DAD: I'm not sure you should know.

ME: I already know, Dad. It is not a secret that I am not your biological child, but I am still your child, and nothing, I mean nothing,
can change that, but this is eating you up inside. I can handle it and
am prepared to know about the past.

DAD: Well, I am just not sure.

ME: Dad, do you know the name of the person?

DAD: Yes.

And there it was: he finally gave me a name, and how it all went down!

He shared with me that he was stationed in North Carolina and
was heading back to Grand Prairie, Texas. He was transported to
Louisiana where he began hitchhiking home. During this timeframe,
he and my mom were divorced but he wanted to get home, see her
and to hold my brother.

Upon arriving at the house, he found a man there named Don.
At that time, I am unaware of what transpired, but I do know she
had a physical relationship with both men, thus my conception. She
convinced my father I was his, they remarried, and I came along. They
divorced again when I was six months old.

When I was a teenager, I recall my mother being angry one day
because I was defending my father to her. She was pissed, and said
he was not as great of a guy as I thought. She told me when she left
my father he replied, "You are taking away the only thing I have truly
ever loved-that little girl!"

In the heat of the moment my mother told him I was not his, so
it did not matter how much he loved me. Some of this is speculation
however, it fits into the timing as to when he learned the truth and

his reasoning for disliking her throughout the years. It was a cruel and horrible thing to do to him but, I wasn't there and did not live with the turbulence between the two of them. These stories surface for almost everyone.

Fortunately, that particular Father's Day ended differently, and the relief I felt is impossible to describe. Words cannot define the overwhelming sensation a Not-Parent Expected child feels at the moment of truth. Obtaining a name was all I needed. It made complete sense because it then connected the last name of Carver across my paternal tree on two DNA sites.

The old adage "The truth will set you free" is powerful in its symbolism and literal meaning. For me, it unlocked the chains of unknowing and the bondage of lies. Honestly, the truth of the matter was only beginning, and freedom is not exactly what was created but it swung the gates of discovery wide open.

Whole

A Broken Heart

A Separated Mind

A Destroyed Bond

All difficult to repair, fix, revive to its past state.

It will never be the same.

Why? Because the damage has been done.

Will I be loved the same again?

Cherished once more?

Or will the love dry up like dust

Absorbed by the wind, never to be obtained again?

We struggle to be whole again

The owner of the bits and pieces is left behind and

Grieves the loss of beauty and perfection that once was.

Time moves forward and suddenly

Each piece begins to fall into place.

The imperfection flaunts its flaws

But the desire to heal is stronger.

Chains of bondage fall away.

The Soul becomes Whole once more.

CHAPTER 14

The Devil is in the Details

Have you ever wondered the origin of the saying "The devil is in the details" and what it actually means? It initiated from the original words "God is in the Details" and transgressed into "The devil is in the details." Loosely translated it means something may seem simple at first glance, but problematic and complex things are always hidden in the details of the situation.

It is so true, as I would quickly learn when I made contact with the first person to actually start providing me details. Once I was armed with a few bits of information, further research assisted in filling in the blanks.

Friends Amongst Strangers

Daniel (not his real name) was the first family member connection I made. He was so kind and helpful during the beginning of my quest to find my biological father and family. Right in my face, front and center on my 23andMe family tree, were mysterious names that had never even been a blip on the radar, but once I had a name it all made sense. This was my first successful dive into finding anyone and it was quickly evident in this adventure I would encounter those who were going to open their hearts and minds and would accept the circumstances. On the other hand, there would be those who would shun me and treat me like some kind of villain and outcast.

Daniel and I spoke for over an hour, and he was full of information. It was like drinking out of a fire hydrant. There were a million details to absorb. Here is what I learned during that first phone conversation.

My bio-father had two siblings, a brother and a sister. The uncle was a writer and published the book *Winnings* along with other literary achievements. Later research would provide information that my aunt was murdered in 2018 on my fifty-fifth birthday, August 31st.

I learned she was a strong businesswoman, owning her own clothing store and was very involved in the community. These were relatable attributes and afforded a feeling of connection for my soul. My birth-father and his wife were also involved in the fashion industry. This was interesting, too because Mom was in the fashionista world for many years as the buyer for a local department store, Watson's.

As an NPE learns more and more the imagination and hopes can run rampant. Dots and pieces begin to connect in the mind whether they are true or not. I was not immune to this "mind tango." Never carry guilt for these imaginings because they are completely normal.

Learning of this aunt's demise saddened me for the family's loss but I also grieved for a woman I would never have the honor to meet. Maybe this sounds weird. How can one grieve for a person they never met?

Let me explain.

Learning you are not who you think you are is troubling, to say the least. Complicate matters with the fact you are fifty-five, and it becomes apparent you are in a race against the clock.

The people you need and want to meet are getting up in years, many are deceased. The truth-Your Truth is passing before your eyes. Desperation sets in and the fear of never learning the entire story grabs your heart. I am not defending whether these emotions are right or wrong. I only know they are real, and no matter how we feel in certain circumstances, it is our right to own those feelings and do with them what we can. Use them to gain more knowledge, shove them in a closet, talk about them or never discuss it, the decision is for each individual to make and no one has the right to deter you from your need to address your heritage.

Daniel told me stories of my grandparents, especially a crucial bit of information about a falling out between my grandmother, Virginia Hall, and her sister-in-law. It seems one or both were very strong-headed, and the disagreement occurred due to some issues surrounding the fashion store they ran together. Details are sketchy, but the story rings true as a distinct possibility to why these different sides of the family did not appear to mix, mingle, or know one another.

In meeting more and more family, it seems this discord filtered through the years. Perhaps this is one of the reasons that half of the family never knew the other half when I mentioned names. Strangely enough, I began to know more family members on each side, and they did not know of the existence of the other half of the family. The half-sisters and cousins denied knowing any of the family members I met and treated me like I was making it all up and lying. This attitude still baffles me because, truly, why on Earth would any sane person do this to themselves? The answer is they wouldn't!

In my first attempt to contact a sister with the knowledge and my mentioning this conflict between the grandmother and aunt actually paused her push back for a short minute. When I asked her if the story rang true, she admitted it did, but as soon as the flash of acceptance appeared it was gone.

She immediately went into a denial state saying, "My father would have never had an affair!" Of course, this was a knee-jerk reaction. Why would she feel this need to get defensive? Fear? Embarrassment? Anger? I was clueless then and am still clueless to this day about the complications she created in her head.

It is difficult to understand why anyone feels the need to defend someone that is no longer around, but it is often a natural reaction. Is it defending their honor or a swift movement to run from reality? Be assured this accusation of an affair was never made by me or part of my side of the conversation. It was totally in her head and made me wonder if there was not an underlying reason for this adamant denial of our bio-father's potential behavior.

There is one undeniable fact: I made a huge mistake in contacting this sister first. In researching the backgrounds of blood relatives this was the person I chose because her Facebook page, her career in helping others, and her social media leaned toward her being accepting. Talk about not being able to judge a book by its cover! What I read (or saw) was not what I got. Not by a long shot. Shame on me for assuming if one was in the business of caring and helping others, they would be open-minded and caring in all situations. It was a true Duh moment.

It was crystal clear I made a huge error in judgment. Her character became more prevalent within a few short days. It did not take long to be forced to step back and reevaluate my strategy. This was not going to work. The one thing she asked was for me to not contact her mother. I held up my part of the bargain but for some weird reason she broke my vow of silence for me and told her mother which by all accounts upset her mother extremely. This in turn got my newfound niece upset with me because "I had upset her grandmother."

Hold on a second. How would I know how to contact her grand-mother? By the way, the word did not come from me and never would. Defending oneself in such an awkward situation is something I would not wish on my worst enemy. You are dumbfounded and, in that moment, it feels like being in a Shakespearian play and "Thou Pro-testeth Too Much." It feels squirmy and the best thing to do was shut my mouth and allow silence to do the talking.

Some of what I would call "insider information," such as the story about my grandmother and her sister-in-law, also became a weapon raised against me in contacting my sisters and cousins. Using the arrows I had been equipped with made me feel like I was in a position to manage the situation. Wouldn't knowing a few true stories be to my advantage? Well, I thought so, but as I brought up names, they all but called me a liar.

Me: Yes, I have been speaking with Daniel, Sharla, Valerie (any name mentioned).

Them: I don't know who that is.

Me: Well, those people are our cousins.

Them: I don't know who you are talking about and I have never met them.

ME THINKING TO MYSELF: That doesn't mean you are not related to them. Then the thoughts became deeper. Maybe there was a reason why they didn't know these people. Maybe that rift was much deeper and wider than anyone realized. It was not my concern or duty to rectify a family at that point. It seemed the damage had been done way before my time of coming on the scene.

It became evident these ladies had their own demons to battle.

Still, I couldn't help but be confused and disheartened by their behavior.

Considering myself to be a realistic and street-smart person it became obvious I needed to take a pause. Had I kidded myself into thinking this was going to be easy? No way! Thinking I was walking into this with eyes wide open is a fair assumption. We know what "assuming" does though and believe me there were moments when assuming made an "ass out of them and me."

Numerous attempts to make contact have fallen short. Sending birthday cards, Mother's Day wishes, and holiday sentiments had failed to stir any response from the four of them. Shame on them is all I can say at this point.

If you are on your own journey or helping someone on their adventure, keep in mind these reactions (or lack thereof) are common and should be expected. My best advice? Toughen up and grow thicker skin before taking a leap of faith expecting you will be welcomed with open arms.

Does it happen? Absolutely! I encounter story after story that solidifies the fact not everyone has to deal with these obnoxious behaviors. However, in most cases, it is my experience seekers encounter their fair share of rejection. This negativity can come from all sides. Lack of support can even be present via a spouse or loved one that does not want to see you hurt. Why? They love you, but maybe it is their hurt they want to avoid. Have a conversation with them. Let them know even though the pain can be unbearable at times it is necessary in order to heal.

Conversations surrounding genetic discovery can be difficult. The seeker often doesn't know what they don't know. These are unchartered waters for everyone involved. It has been discussed in prior chapters. There is no manual, guidebook, or roadmap to assist in this endeavor.

Hopefully, as time marches on there will be more options to better equip oneself in handling this journey. It would make life much easier for many. That is my desire for this book. Hopefully, it will open more minds and hearts to the possibilities and to embrace the unknown. God put all of us here for a reason. Who are we to question His motive for doing so?

Whatever your faith, beliefs, or spiritual inclinations, have you found any religious teachings that stress hatred toward fellow woman/ man, mistreatment of another, or encouraging anyone to be judge and jury here on Earth? I didn't think so.

What Have I Accomplished?

On the surface, it seems like nothing.
I've moved no mountains   I've gained no traction
I haven't profited from others' pain, despair or agony.
But what I have accomplished is beyond the force of nature.
I have accomplished
      Sunshine
I have gained
      Happiness
I have succeeded
      With the help of friends
I have become a force
      The person I was before
      Lost for a time, but found again
A person to be reckoned with,
      A life to be enjoyed
      Like the pounding of a wave crashing on the beach
      The warmth of the sun hitting my cheeks
Hearing the power
      Feeling the beat
Being alone with the ebb
Feeling strength in the tide
Biggest accomplishment?
Learning to be Me, a force on my own.

CHAPTER 15

This Shit is Getting Real

As mentioned before when making the first initial contact with my half-sister she was slightly rude, but I accepted it as shock. I felt momentary relief when she offered the assistance of someone that understood genealogy. Little did I know it was a set-up. She and her friend, Jena, offered to help but the underlying goal was to disprove me and by no means to encourage the search.

Their behavior can only be defined as pure evil. Here I was vulnerable and showing my hand while they were concocting a plan against my discovery. My trust even went so far as to share my passwords so they could help me. I can hear you now saying how dumb this was. I am well aware it was, and hindsight is 20/20. Shit hit the fan, though, when I reached out to the other half-sister. The promise was that I would not contact their mother. Never did I commit to not contacting other family members.

The other half-sister notified these two conspirators about my message. Then they started sending me hateful texts, took down their Facebook pages and began harassing me. It seemed a bit extreme to go to all this trouble because of one phone call and one message on Ancestry but it was exactly their reaction. I knew the existence of any kindness or help was out the door.

The positive outcome of the entire incident was she and her friend introduced a foreign topic to me—Centimorgans. Well, now I was curious. What was a centimorgan and how do I determine them? What do they mean?

A centimorgan (cM) is a fancy way geneticists use to describe the length of DNA segments. The meaning in the DNA world describes how much DNA we share with other people. We share varying sizes and segments of DNA with relatives. A centimorgan measures genetic distance. We each have approximately 6800 cM of DNA. Therefore, we have approximately 3400 cM from each parent. The higher the cM with another person the closer in relation we are to them.

Each measurement of a cM has a specific length. The length of the DNA segment provides clues as to how distant the ancestor. People distantly related will have small segments in common.

Size Matters

Size is significant in the DNA segmentation. The longer the segment you share with a person the closer in relationship they are to you. In my case, I had a cM value of 3,200 with my mom and a gentleman came up with approximately 1,600. Later, this man was determined to be my uncle. In addition to this, I had a cM number that placed me as half-siblings with two women and first cousins with another woman. It boiled down to simple mathematics, and facts are stubborn things. They don't lie! My sister and her friend seemed to believe the cM numbers were going to clench their belief I was not legitimate. Surprise, surprise the numbers didn't lie and they inadvertently helped me uncover the facts I was seeking.

The cM numbers pointed directly toward blood relatives. Now it is funny these two thought they were going to steer me off path, but in actuality, they opened the floodgates of relatives. When it was happening, it hurt like hell but now I am forever thankful to them for showing me the way.

Centimorgans in Your Face!

In a conversation with one cousin, she stated, "I have no doubt my father is your uncle."

She was a follower of Ancestry and pretty savvy. At first, she was excited to meet me. That is until my sister jumped in and began contacting immediate family members and asked them to not communicate with me. The fortunate part of my scenario was these defensive members of my biological father's side of the family did not seem to know or acknowledge much of the other family members. Thus, they were never able to taint them against me. Whatever conflict occurred and created this division within the family was not forthcoming, but it was obvious something had happened many years ago and it caused various groups to go separate ways. I may never know the truth but I will continue to ask the questions.

At the publication of this book none of these women of my immediate family or their children(two half-sisters, three nephews, and two first cousins) have accepted my existence nor our undeniable relationship. To say it got nasty is an understatement and was completely unexpected.

Recently, I sent both sisters a loving and genuine note and they both scribbled out their names and sent the notes back to me with "Return to Sender." These reactions and unacceptable treatment were the catalyst and purpose for sharing my story. They never realized it added fuel to the fire, and did not squelch the flame in my belly for the facts and desire to connect.

First, if you are a person being introduced to an NPE, please think of how you can be hurting a person that did not ask for this. Secondly, if you are a person stepping out to seek the truth be mentally and emotionally prepared for the "what ifs." They will happen.

Remember the Seinfeld episode when George uses the breakup plan of "It's not you it's me?" Well, in this world of DNA surprises, if someone acts unjustly to you go watch this episode, laugh out loud and accept the fact that "It's not you, it's them." In other words, this is their issue, not yours. Move on to find other relatives that will gladly open their arms to you. For most people, family is everything. Embrace this knowledge and look for others in your lifeline. As far as the haters, let them hate and refuse to let them bring you down. This is your time to learn and shine so please don't let anyone take away the joy that is possible with your discovery.

All I can say to the naysayers is this: I truly hope you or a family member never needs a kidney or blood transfusion, and I am your only hope. It puts a very different light on all this acceptance stuff when you look at it that way. It may sound a bit callous but ignoring your own flesh and blood is about as callous as you can get in life.

This shit is for real and the approach an NPE takes in addressing the situation is paramount in the outcome. As you will hear me say often, "this does not just affect us as NPEs." It affects numerous people so being prepared with the introduction and understanding the potential outcomes should serve everyone positively, if possible. We cannot control the reactions of others, but we have absolute control of how we act and react to the circumstances as they unravel.

CHAPTER 16

Rocking the Italian Boat— Annie's Story

Including other people's stories is meant to help understand there are many ways DNA awareness occurs and to help everyone realize this situation is becoming more common every day in our society. The goal is to help NPEs know they are not alone. This is a scary new world for many of us and it is vital to comprehend there are others out in the world going through the same hurts, thrills, and anxiety DNA Surprises can bring. There are times when friends and family feel like they need a whiteboard and a flow chart when NPEs tell their stories. Don't worry as you are around it more and more the pieces start to click into place. Annie's story has some moving parts, but the main thing is to enjoy her tale of adventure and have fun along the way.

A big thank you to Annie for sharing her story.

Enjoy!

> *I've been doing genealogy as a hobby since 2000 when the Ellis Island records first came online. I was thirty-nine years old and half Irish/half Italian. My dad's parents were "off the boat" from Naples, so I was pretty excited to learn more about my heritage. I never knew my Italian grandparents, but I was raised with my dad's*

Italian family and if asked, I'd usually say, "I'm Italian . . . well, half Irish" because I didn't even know my mom's side of the family. I considered myself Italian. I was so intrigued when I looked at all those ship manifests and so thrilled to find my grandmother—little ten-year-old Guiseppa, her four sisters, and their mother. It was 1903. I just stared at that manifest and marveled at their bravery; a woman my same age, thirty-nine-years-old, and her five little girls, all travelling alone to a new country where their husband and father waited for them. Wow!

Fast forward to 2012. Ancestry was coming out with a new at-home DNA test, and it could connect me with unknown relatives. They were offering subscribers first crack at their new product once it was available. A few months later, I was able to order my test. I spit in the tube and waited. Then the email arrived saying my results were ready. Eagerly logging into Ancestry, I saw names of people and the breakdown of my ethnicity. Looking at names, I recognized no one. Then I looked at the ethnicity results. Wait! Why did that say I'm 98 percent Irish? What does that mean? Where was all my Italian? I really didn't understand any of this, so I told myself that there must not be a big database for them to draw from. Surely once more people tested, that would change. I pretty much went back to my research and tree work and barely thought about it. Occasionally, I'd go back and look at my matches and I still didn't see any familiar names or any Italian. Anyone I could ask was long since deceased.

In 2015, I received a message from a woman named Shannon. I hadn't looked at my results in a while, so I opened the message and read that she looked at my tree and was puzzled. She couldn't figure out how I fit into her tree. We matched at 291 centimorgans (cMs), which I now know is a good match, first cousin once removed or second cousin. I went to Shannon's tree and saw nearly 3,000 strangers. I looked at our shared matches and saw more strangers.

I also looked at my ethnicity again and still not a single drop of Italian. Writing back to Shannon, I explained to her that I couldn't figure out where I fit in her tree. However, if I came across new information, I'd reach out to her.

It was at this point I started thinking something was terribly awry. Was it possible that my mother cheated on my dad? Nah, it couldn't possibly be. That wasn't like her. There must have been a mistake in the test. So, I did what so many others do in my position. I called Ancestry to give them a piece of my mind! I got someone on the phone and asked them about the accuracy of the test and questioned whether there could be an error. I was told their test is 99.9 percent accurate. I was stunned.

I grew up with one brother and one sister; my brother died in 2006. I told my sister about my test results and asked her if she would do a test for me. She was completely intrigued and said she'd test. In telling a friend about my test, she suggested 23andMe. I'd never heard of them but went online and ordered a test. My sister's test came back. I opened Ancestry to look at her results—48 percent Irish, 46 percent Italian/Western Europe. More importantly, our cMs were 2,001. She was my half-sister. Shortly after that, I got my 23andMe results back, which gave me 99 percent Irish and another crowd of strangers who were related to me. I had the proverbial needle in a haystack.

In September 2017, a first cousin match appeared on Ancestry. I couldn't believe it! I thought I finally might get some answers. The match's name was Ed. I immediately sent a message to Ed and explained I received some unusual results on my DNA test. I asked him if his mother had any brothers. Ed responded right away. His mother had two brothers. They were both priests! No way! Even though I was raised Catholic, my mom NEVER went to church. When was she going to be able to have a social relationship with a priest while working *full-time and two little kids at home? Ed told me he had a tree, but that his sister knew more than he did. He asked his sister to get me names, dates, and relationships. I went and looked at Ed's tree and saw the two priests there, one born in 1900 and the other born in 1910. My mom was born in 1928, so this was quite an age difference, but who knows? Then I saw some other names that looked familiar. Suddenly I remembered Shannon from 2015, and wasn't her last name the one I saw on Ed's tree? I went back to Shannon's tree and some of Ed's people appeared! Could this be the key?*

By now, I had names from Ed's sister, and I could see Shannon's tree, so I asked Ed if he knew Shannon. He said, "Yes, I do, we're second cousins." OMG! Now I had a breakthrough. I was able to figure out Ed and Shannon weren't really cousins. They weren't even blood-related. But for my purposes, this was perfect. Ed's aunt, Aileen, was married to Shannon's father's brother (uncle), Jack. Jack and Aileen were my grandparents. Jack and Aileen had three sons and two daughters, so one of these sons was my birthfather. Now how to figure out which one? For the most part, my mystery was solved. Two of the three brothers were dead; both sisters were still alive. Ed and I exchanged numerous emails. He shared with me that he and his wife spent winters in Florida, where the oldest of Jack and Aileen's children lived with her daughter. This would be my Aunt Jackie, and my cousin Keira.

Ed told me while he and his wife were in Florida, they'd visit several times with Jackie and Keira, and he would gently bring me up. Eventually, he took Keira aside and told her the whole story. He gave Keira my email and we started corresponding and speaking on the phone. This was in early 2018, and on Easter of that year, Ed and his wife went to Jackie and Keira's for dinner. It just so happened that one of Keira's cousins was there, a daughter of one of the three brothers. I had given Ed a lot of information about my mom, like where she worked when I was conceived, she was on a bowling league, and some other stuff.

During this particular visit, they all started chatting about the old days. Ed's wife brought up the cousin's dad and said, "Oh, didn't he work at IBM?" She said, "No, he worked at S&V." Ed and his wife told me later it was all they could do to not explode because they knew that my mom worked at S&V. So, my needle in a haystack was solved. All this dropped into my lap in a matter of a few days.

Since that fateful Easter, I have met and become very close with the people in this story. I have six siblings from my birthfather, but my new siblings have not been willing to speak to me except one brother, but it's usually me who initiates contact. Of my birthfather's seven kids, I am smack in the middle and could be considered an Irish triplet—one brother is nine months older than me, and one brother is ten months younger than me.

So that's my story.

If you made it this far, thanks for sticking with it. Trust me when I say if I tell it in person, it's a lot longer—I got my rambling storytelling ability from my father, along with his quiet love of reading, his cheeks, and his freckles. I just wish I would have been able to meet him. Aunt Jackie said I look just like him and she said, "he'd have loved me."

Thanks again to Annie for sharing her story. It reminds me how this journey is filled with highs and lows. It is like solving a mystery in most cases and the NPE is the detective coming upon clue after clue. Some witnesses are helpful and others stonewall the investigation. Each piece of the puzzle that fits into place brings the NPE closer to resolution. Viewing this like a whodunit makes dealing with the enigma much more fun.

CHAPTER 17

Confrontation—Walk Softly & Carry a Big Stick

This is my disclaimer chapter. It had to happen. Inevitably, a group of readers, people, critics will dislike this book and rage on about how I have misguided you or defend the stance that seekers do not have the right to ask the questions. They will hold the position that it disrupts lives and therefore, should not be allowed.

There is no reason to speak my piece about this mindset. It is evident how I think and feel on this topic, so here goes my shot at altruistic guidance. Maybe, just maybe, it will keep the wolves at bay.

Secluding myself while writing has been a habit and escape for many years. It is appropriate that while writing this "disclaimer chapter" jazz music plays in the background, a soft breeze blows on a lazy day in June and a summer rain starts wafting the smell of grass and the promise of Texas heat to come shortly. The thunder rolls around me symbolically ushering in the lightening that follows. The discourse between seekers of the truth and those that want to quelch that thirst because they "can't handle the truth" is evident and unyielding. Sadly, a storm will be part of the controversy. DNA surprises and discoveries are not immune to the ridicule of others.

It takes strength, wherewithal, grit, passion, and a little bit of innocence to jump on this Train of Truth. It is not for the faint of heart because there are times where it will rip your heart out with the things people say and do. Things you could and would have never imagined.

Fear not! You got this! You need supporters so start developing your tribe as early as possible. Make sure they can stand the heat. If not, they do not need to be in this kitchen with you. It can get really hot and at times steamy. Like a good *sous-chef*, they need to have your back and help you prep for the tasty and savory future you have coming your way.

Some days you will need a fork and knife, others a spoon but there is no doubt there will be times you need a (chop) stick, a Big Ass Stick. Theodore Roosevelt has always been my favorite president. Don't ask me why. Maybe it was his big macho self, or that he minced no words, a straight shooter telling it the way it was: strong, bold, and honest. All admirable traits in a human and leader.

Roosevelt cultivated the "Big Stick Ideology." He described it as the "exercise of intelligent forethought and of decisive action sufficiently far in advance of any likely crisis."

Roosevelt's policy had five components. These components still stand as a solid strategy to this day. It is a strategy utilizing diplomacy which can prove helpful in the DNA game plan.

The five components are as follows:

1. It is essential to possess serious military capability. Remember what I said about getting supporters around you. There will be times when you feel you are going into battle. Outsiders to the DNA surprise world may never understand these feelings of apprehension, but they can be real and raw emotions that can overwhelm.

2. Act Justly. It goes without saying we need to treat others with compassion. This is all a shock to them, too (well, in most cases).

3. Never Bluff. If you bluff, be prepared to deal with the ramifications. An example of bluffing might be threatening to post the news all over social media. Slander and libel are real, so, make sure you have your facts straight before making a move.

4. Strike only when prepared to strike hard. This goes back to number three. Know those cM numbers and make sure they are accurate. Arm yourself with stories from others if possible. If you are throwing out potential scenarios, make sure they have substance.

5. Be willing to allow the adversary to save face in defeat. None of us are here on this journey to embarrass, injure, or demean anyone. If you are, then I beseech you to rethink your stance and purpose. You may be hurt, angry and downright ticked off but this is the time to be the "the bigger person." If rejection is front and center, then move out of the way and let it take the stage. By showing grace and empathy you will hopefully gain the same from others. You will rarely win if you come in with both barrels loaded.

The idea considers negotiating peacefully but also having strength with facts, knowledge, and irrefutable purpose in case things go wrong. And be aware things could go wrong, but that is OK because you are prepared for the various outcomes.

Old cliches about coming hard and fast come to mind when considering the behavior of many learning the truth about their biological life. Like a "bull in a china shop" identifies a person who breaks things or who often makes mistakes or causes damage in situations that should require careful thinking before acting.

This discovery and approaching others with the recently-gained knowledge is a precarious dance. Everyone has an opinion of how it should be handled. As discussed before, there is no right, or wrong way specifically set in stone in how to best proceed in addressing others.

It is like any delicate matter in life. The approach needs to be well thought out, and how it will affect others should be high priority. Before jumping in with both feet, I studied individuals and their backgrounds as much as possible. Preparing questions with a gentle attitude was the main focus. Not always easy to do, but it is important if you want to get anywhere.

Being in sales my entire life afforded me a strong understanding of rejection and that "no" is not personal, and it is only "no" for now. However, if I am being honest, and I always want to be honest with you, the negative actions of the first family members ticked me off. There its out there! It was personal when they started twisting the story and ignoring the details and facts placed in front of them. Denying the truth with accusations could make the strongest of people upset. It hurts and it should hurt. We are all human with feelings and insecurities.

Yes, it is apparent to me that I had more time to process, think about it, and compose myself. The fact remains that rejection is always difficult to absorb, especially when all you want is compassion and understanding. There are some things maybe I should have done differently, but I'm not sure what it would actually look like if I went back in time and recalculated the events. It was handled the best way I knew how under the circumstances. That is all any of us can do.

Every time in meeting new family members I experience a bit of trepidation with butterflies in my stomach, their wings fluttering around my insides to make sure I am paying attention. Those flutters keep me in check and make sure that each and every moment of this journey is a delicate waltz, with some tango and cha cha cha thrown in for good measure, keeping me on my toes.

If you have these feelings, embrace them. Flight or fight? I say fight with the most subtle and gentle motives. Keep in mind, if the stick you are carrying is way too big you could create the flight characteristic in another. There will be enough scampering away without adding more distress into the mix.

Walk softly but carry a big stick. Do not retreat at the first sign of battle and prepare for the potentiality of a fight. Decide ahead of time how you will handle various scenarios, and always remember: You are not a Dirty Little Secret and you have the right to know your past!

CHAPTER 18

Obituaries are Your Friend

You may or may not be interested in searching for family members from your past, present and well, we know your future is out of the question. However, if you are starting a search, obituaries are your friend.

They are a treasure chest in finding people.

Let me elaborate on this odd line of thinking.

We all probably know someone who avidly reads the obituaries. Some think this is a morbid habit and I tend to agree. There was once a woman working for me and reading the obits was the first thing she did every morning. It seemed strange in the beginning. However, as time went by it proved to be very helpful in the insurance industry because she would find things when they happened to our valued customers. It was a great way to keep up with the community and be able to reach out to people and show we cared.

Years later, obituaries proved to be a different asset when looking for my biological family. In the DNA search, obituaries are potentially one of the most valuable records available to vet the past.

Obits can provide a plethora of information and they come in many forms. Early in the 1800s, newspapers would post death notices. These notices were maybe a couple of sentences.

Over time notices became lengthier and included much more detail. The 1900s brought about the publishing of more descriptive obituaries which we are familiar with today. Google, Yahoo, and Bing are valuable sources in the search for obits, often leading straight to the source or opening other avenues to follow. If you are seeking connections to other family members these small synopses can be a goldmine.

They can provide:

Place of birth

Death date & place

Age of the deceased

Spouses' names and possibly place of marriage

Insights into ancestors' lives such as where they worked, hobbies, things they loved

Reason or cause of death

And of course, the most vital of all: Names of family members who have passed before or those still alive. These are especially important, as you can imagine, because they create an opportunity to contact these people to hopefully ascertain more data. However, as discussed in different chapters the seeker needs to be prepared for rejection and the reaction of those who are just learning the truth, too. These names can provide extraordinary clues to other records and connections.

Cause of death was a huge moment for me because it identified the fact my bio dad died of leukemia after a short battle fighting the disease. He was only sixty years old. This is pretty damned important news. Since no one in my immediate family had ever been diagnosed with leukemia this was good to know. It turned my medical tables upside down and provided a knowledge of a potential health risk I never would have imagined.

While searching for my father, the information of my aunt's demise also came to light. In my heart, I had such high hopes of getting to meet her, but the hope was dashed when I came upon her death notice. Yet, it opened more areas to search. Sadly, the digging brought me to the article about her murder in 2018. My heart fell realizing I would never be fortunate enough to meet her. As time has evolved and more about her has come to light, her loss is even sadder than when I first learned of her unfortunate demise. It was the loss of an incredible woman: a woman I would love to have known.

Family members say I look and act a lot like her and my paternal grandmother. This may not seem like much to some people but for those of us learning about a family we never met it becomes a lifeline of love, hope and compassion.

More recently, my investigation led me to learn my paternal grandfather died of cancer at the age of seventy-five and my grandmother suffered from Alzheimer's and passed in 1997 at the age of eight-two.

Death is never a fun topic, but the great part is that these memorials can give us insight into the people making up our own DNA. Some fun tidbits I have been told are:

My grandmother and aunt both loved fashion and owned their own businesses—Check.

My aunt loved animals—Check.

My grandmother was a great basketball player—Check.

She loved softball and played at every position—Check.

She also loved people, was a natural born salesperson, adored music and laughter—Check, Check, and Check.

It may seem odd, but I cherish and relish this information because they all define the things I care about and love, too. It was a connection for me and answered a lot of "where did I get this from? Why do I feel this way, act this way, or have this talent?"

Strangely, the family I grew up with hold very few of these characteristics in life. Well, except Fashion, which my mother was amazing at and was exceptionally talented. Humor has always been an escape from a tough or awkward situation for me. Now it seems I truly came by it naturally. Some things are taught, and some are just in the genes. I am blessed to have a part of many amazing people in my life and in my genetic makeup.

Getting back to the importance of obituaries let me share more of what it provided. One of my best friends discovered my biological father's obituary, and it led me to learn I had two half-sisters, three nephews, and a niece living in the same area. We had been living in the same city and in close vicinity all our lives and never knew it! I could not believe it. It also unraveled the discovery of a gentleman I had known and done business with for the previous twenty years to be my ex-bother-in-law. We certainly have had a few laughs over this detail. This very general information can open door-after-door for the seeker or for someone collaborating with them on their journey.

One of the greatest things about these little nuggets is they give amazing clues to other records which can signal a check of data, such as military background, religious involvement, community, and the ancestor's way of life.

You get the idea. Will every turn produce the results you desire? Probably not, but this provides ideas and a foundation of where to begin a search. One thing will lead to another, and at times it leads to a closed door, but there are numerous paths available to move things along.

Next on my DNA bucket list? Visiting my ancestors' gravesites. It feels like it will be a connection to my heart and soul, and is truly needed. Through death we often find life. Life is a gift given to us by these amazing ancestors we so feverishly seek to find.

CHAPTER 19

Letter to the Father I Never Met

Dear Dad,

Well, here we are, two total strangers, yet I am part of you and you of me. I can only hope you and Mom are in Heaven and had a conversation about what happened. In your conversation, my prayer is that you can both look over me here on Earth and have my back together. I can only laugh and grin at how the discussions are going up there with all my loved ones. I would love to be the fly on that cloudy Heavenly wall.

In my heart-of-hearts I truly believe you never knew about me. Maybe it is just the little girl in me hoping you never did. Then there would be a reason why you never tried to come find or meet me. So far, all the things I have learned creates the belief you and my grandparents were good people and, if any of you had ever known, you would have tried to connect. Of course, I could be wrong, but a girl can dream.

Or maybe you did know and were too kind, afraid, or wrapped up in your life and family that you felt you could not do anything about it. At this point it really doesn't matter.

However, I must admit the immediate family you left behind, my two half-sisters, and your brother and sister's daughters have not been very kind nor accepting. It has not been an easy journey with them though I have tried to communicate and meet them on numerous occasions.

It is so strange. I cannot for the life of me figure out what they are afraid of. If you can soften their hearts and you and your mom and dad could place your hands on them to open their minds, it would be greatly appreciated. I am not trying to rock their world or change who you are in their eyes. All I want is a chance to know more about you and the man that you were here on Earth. My understanding is you were very witty and laughed a lot. Recently, I discovered you loved Dr. Pepper, smoked, and had a flat top haircut. This vision makes me laugh out loud because these are things, I never grew up around.

On the positive side of the family, our distant relatives and cousins have been amazing. We have met and I have spent time with them, and it revives my soul and outlook, reminding me there are good people out there and they want to help. They could not be more loving and have accepted me with open arms. I am sure you can look down and see this crazy world and wonder what is going on with everyone. Yet, one thing coming from all the crazy is a philosophy and mindset of inclusion, acceptance, and diversity. This awesome side of the family is all these things and I am so thankful because they have helped ease the pain of those that have rejected me.

Seems there was lots of turmoil and differences amongst family members over the years, but isn't it the truth for most all families? But as I meet more and more of the family and hear the stories, it helps me better understand the fear of my sisters and cousins. Stepping back, I realize I don't know the past hurts and complications causing their reaction. There are times when it is best to leave well enough alone and let sleeping dogs lie.

That is hard for me because hey, I am a Carver by blood, and what I have learned thus far is that Carvers are strong-headed and do not give up easily. I was raised this way too by my parents but there is no doubt I have my father's blood. Your mom and dad sound like they were exceptional humans from all I have read and heard. Your brother and sister both credit them with being extremely loving and giving in the books they published. Did I tell you I am a writer, too? Yep, the fruit seems to have fallen pretty close to the tree! Cousins have told me how much I look and act like Carvers through my actions, laughter and mannerisms. That gives me great pride. You know I always wondered where my nose came from. Now I know!

I am sure you are already aware (all of you guys being in Heaven together) I was raised by remarkable people, and they loved me immensely. At times it makes this journey even harder because I never want to hurt the people who gave me their all. Yet, it can never remove the feeling something is missing. And the something is you and the family I never had the opportunity to know.

Would it have changed anything? Maybe, maybe not. All I know is how I feel and the hole in my heart. A hole that was created by people who loved me, and I loved and trusted them. A hole that I try to fill by meeting new family members. Maybe I am chasing a dream, an illusion or I am flat out delusional, but it is my fantasy.

Chasing this fantasy helps me to heal. So, I will continue to run after my dream and no one else has the right to tell me I should not or cannot do it. It is mine and I own it, especially since so many others did not and do not want to accept my existence.

Thank you for giving me life even though you didn't know you did (again I am sticking with this being the story). My past, present, and future are fulfilling and wonderful. I have no regrets except I never had the opportunity to meet *you!* I turn sixty this year. The same age you were when you passed from leukemia. Though it is so sad you left this world too early and we never had the chance to meet, I am so thankful I was able to learn the reason for losing you. Like any daughter, I pray I would have made you proud!

Tell Mom the "cat's out of the bag" and everyone down here will know the truth when this book is published, and it is okay because she was the best mom ever. She just needed to come clean a little earlier in life so we could have met. Like most children I will always love you, unconditionally. If I could have changed the situation, I promise, I would have.

Farewell until Later.

Your Loving Daughter,
Lezlee

CHAPTER 20

Blood is Thicker Than Water—NOT!

Another cliché for you to wonder about and for me to share. Ever wonder where this old cliché came from? And what it means?

The most common meaning for the proverb "Blood is Thicker Than Water" is that **family relationships and familial bonds are stronger than friendships, influential relationships, and links.**

By now I am sure you are aware I cannot disagree more with this statement or the meaning of the proverb in the DNA context! All the people mentioned in prior chapters raised me. They are my family, and no matter the outcome will always be important to me, and nothing changes this going forward.

I was raised by my stepdad since I was three and he loved me like I was well, excuse me for saying it-his own blood. The man I believed to be my biological father throughout life continued to treat me as though I was . . . yep, you guessed it, his own flesh and blood. The irony here is that neither of them were my biological parent, but they both treated me with love and kindness. They never questioned my heritage or who I was as a child or the adult I would become.

Let's delve into this old saying a bit further.

Blood is, in fact, thicker or more viscous (sticky, gummy) than water. But the phrase "blood is thicker than water" has nothing to do with the consistency of either substance.

Consider the word thick first.

The dictionary defines it as: "the busiest or most crowded part of something; the middle of something"

So, when we think in terms of this saying it makes sense blood is thicker and therefore is more important to the bond. Digging deeper provides the common uses of the word "thick" when it comes to friendships and other non-blood relationships.

You have heard these sayings I am sure:

"Thick as thieves"
"Through thick and thin"
"In the thick of things"

So, the idiom can mean something completely different than just being close and bonded through genetics, blood, and DNA. Most of us have people in our lives who are not a sibling, parent, grandparent, aunt, or uncle. We are closer to them out of pure friendship and bonds that bind us together.

As we look at the saying "blood is thicker than water" again, we can picture this thick, slow-moving liquid. It pools and starts to stagnate and congeal. Our imagination takes us to what we see in movies and television shows. Thank goodness many of us have never seen that kind of bloody scene. Yet, those images remain with us and as we compare this image to the flow of water, we see the fast, moving and potentially destructive action of water.

Now you have this picture in your mind let me blow up the myth of what the term really means. The original saying was first written in the Bible. It says, "blood of the covenant is thicker than the water of the womb". Over time the original words "covenant" and "womb" were dropped.

"Covenant" is a strong word for an official agreement or promise. This term in the Bible-based idiom translates into the covenant between soldiers in battle. Their promise to take care of one another is stronger than water. This promise is "thick" to say the least. In better understanding the true meaning we realize the idiom has been changed over history to mean something entirely different than the first interpretation.

The cliche has been highly debated over time. The oldest record of this saying can be traced back to the twelfth century in Germany and it seems the meaning has taken on a life of its own through the years.

Regardless of who first recorded it, some believe the expression came from the idea water evaporates without leaving traces, while blood leaves a stain and evidence behind. Therefore, it appears to be more potent and durable. We know blood leaves a stain. Maybe this is why in theory it is intended to "bond us together."

Blood is intended to tie people together but when we have been denied this covenant with family members these secrets begin to prove "blood is not thicker than water." The promise to keep the lies and deception becomes stronger than the covenant of shared heritage. With that said, we know that learning the truth does not cleanse away the stains of secrecy. In fact, it opens wounds that will bleed for longer than we can fathom.

The moments of pain can appear when least expected. This is true in all walks-in-life, not just in DNA discovery. Plenty of people discover unfaithful partners. Learning the truth does not cleanse the hurt and pain of the adultery. The truth can often be more painful than staying in the dark when it comes to the actions of others. Especially, when those actions directly affect us.

Lastly, it is interesting to embrace the fact that blood and water have many of the same characteristics and functions in our body. They are necessary to our health and life.

Blood and water share these commonalities:

- They are both necessary for survival

- Each delivers oxygen to the body

- They assist in flushing out toxins

- Both are transporters of nutrients to the cells

In a nutshell, they are both equally important. It is just as important in our day-to-day life to have relationships with loved ones carrying our same blood and those who do not.

As previously mentioned, I love using music to help me understand myself, and when I absorb the lyrics and their meanings it helps me look at situations in a different light. There are two excellent songs entitled "Blood is Thicker Than Water." One is by Sonny Bazini (I love his unique voice) and the other is by Black Label Society. This one is a little harder rock, but the words strike a chord.

Reflecting upon the words, the depth of the covenant and promise of friendship stands out in support of the extremes we will suffer for those we love. Reflect on the people walking with you on this journey whether they have the same blood as you or not. It doesn't matter, because all that truly matters is the person and what they mean to you. Through thick or thin are they there for you? If they are then count yourself lucky and work on cultivating more relationships just like it.

Final Thoughts

No matter where you are from or how you arrived at this point in life, be confident in the fact that you are here for a purpose. Each of us has a purpose! My entire life I have prayed for God to show me a way to help others and to guide me toward my Purpose. Through this DNA discovery, it seems as though my prayers have been answered.

It is obvious there is so much still to do in the DNA surprise and NPE world.

Most of the time it seems answers never come fast enough or in a way that I want things to happen. I push and shove, trying to fit the round pegs into square holes. There are times of success and times of failure. We all have those moments, but I encourage you to stay your course. It may take you in many directions. There is one thing I devoutly believe, and that is God (or the Higher Being you believe in) wants you to get up and get moving toward your Purpose.

Yes, we can "Place it in God's hands" but He/She expects us to put in the work it takes to be successful in any endeavor. No matter our spiritual walk, we all stumble, question, and flat out walk away at times. There is absolutely nothing wrong with doing that! It means we are growing. Most importantly though, as we have heard a million and one times, we must get back up and face the challenges before us. For there is nothing like humility and failure to make us stronger.

Stay resilient and steadfast and hold on to the knowledge that you have the right to challenge, investigate and search for your own truth. It belongs to you. There will be those people who want to squelch and treat you like you are an interloper. It can make you feel self-conscious and insecure, but I encourage you to hold your head high and enjoy this ride. It is your water bucket to carry and your blood to shed. Bottomline, the choice in how you take on any battle is up to you. Make your choices be for the good whenever possible and love every chance you get.

The Time Will Come

When I look back at an adventure with people, complete
   strangers that are now a part of my life-past, present,
   and future. A time will come when I share with each
   of them words or an action I noticed, some small
   intricacies.

Listening when they did not think I heard, observing when
   they did not think I watched. Learning minute details
   of behavior, attitude, likes, dislikes . . . how they take
   their coffee, vegan or meat eater, no nuts or nuts, dairy
   products, responses, moods, feelings . . . .

The time will come when this information will be important
   to me, maybe to them.

Breathing

Listening

Watching

Awareness

Learning from others before me and after.

The time will come when the differences amongst us will fill
   the gaps for others.

Bonded

     Six Degrees

        Separation

           Entwined

              Knowing

                 No Escape

                    Eternity

CHAPTER 21

Sisterhood

What is the definition of "Sisterhood?" It means various things to different people. It is the state of being a sister, a community or society of sisterhood, or the solidarity of women based on shared conditions, experiences, or concerns.

My life has always been full of amazing women. Growing up with no sister, the words sisters and sisterhood had little meaning to me. However, in joining a sorority in college this changed and the definition of "sister" took on an entirely new concept. The term sisterhood encapsulates an unconditional alliance between like-minded (and not-so-like-minded) individuals. These people empower and lift one another up.

Of course, substitute the words "brother" and "brotherhood" and it can carry the same connotation. As humans we construct these bonds, we become stronger as we become part of a unit. A unit affording the opportunity to belong and be a part of a unique group.

Sisterhood pushes and breaks ties binding us to the old belief a sister only exists if you share the same blood. This is not exactly the truth. It is more than friendship; it is a bond that is forever and survives many phases of life. A true sister celebrates the happy times and is there to comfort, love, and support you during the rough times, too.

This is not a fair-weathered friend. It is a friend who will go to battle for you even when they don't have a dog in the fight. This person may question your sanity and decisions, but once they understand your need, agenda, and goal they never turn back.

During this DNA journey my sisterhood and brotherhood has made me reconsider the importance of these bonds. The power of these relationships has always been a paramount element in my life. It provides a strength that cannot be obtained on my own. I need it and want to be a part of a community that loves me and wants to see me succeed. This holds true for the people in my Life Community.

So many people have lost their families, never knew their family, or have just outright dissolved familial ties. Through death or decision there is an ebb and flow of people in and out of our lives. Some people we miss and wish we still had them to hug and share our latest story. Others have been in our lives for a reason, or a season and it is for the best when they move on.

It has always been important to surround myself with a diverse group. I have loud friends and quiet friends (not that many but I do have a few), fixers, messer-uppers, artists, writers, engineers, sales reps, account managers, retirees, great cooks, non-cooks, talkers, listeners, Christians, Buddhist, Muslims, politicians, restaurant owners, entrepreneurs, and developers all included in this repertoire of stupendous people I am lucky enough to call friends.

Interestingly, they are more than friends. I love them deeply and dearly and consider them family. There are blood ties, genetic ties, long-term relationships and those with whom bonds were developed later in life. As we open our hearts, anyone can discover a larger family and it does not need to include DNA connections. These relationships have taken on a special reason and need for me, especially, after the way my two newly found sisters and two cousins have turned the other way and have chosen a path of unacceptance. Somewhere deep inside there is a reason they refuse to see the real person standing in front of them.

I don't do "mean girls" very well, especially since my life is so full of the most interesting, courageous, loyal, and honest people. They represent the pillars of my personal foundation. Why would anyone want to subject themselves to "mean anything?" Have I given up hope one sister might decide to see things differently than her older sister, or one of my cousins might realize I am no threat and merely want a connection? No, I have not given up that hope. However, whether they do or do not eventually change their minds, it will not and does not define me. But, again, it is not all about me.

It is important to keep in mind the effect that these discoveries have on others, even when we want to shout from the rooftops or shake the crap out of someone until they get a clue. I would bet every person that has had an NPE experience or has found a secret from their past has felt this way at one point or another. It is natural. It is reality. So please, hold onto the drive and desire to continue your search.

Open to the possibilities of meeting a new person every day (or week if that is too overwhelming). Maybe they become a force in your life or maybe not, but you are growing with each step you take, every hand you shake, or neck you hug. These interactions bring you closer to building a family that is yours forever if you chose to make it happen. The bonds we nurture and support will strengthen our well-being by reducing stress levels and ultimately improving mental health. These ties can empower and inspire each of us. Hey, it if can do all these things then it is certainly worth a try.

We can have a kinship with those we have never met. We share the same emotions, experiences, and revelations with so many others even if we live worlds apart. As we study genealogy, it is possible to see our past and garner the history of those that came before us, and the hardships they faced. They may not have had to determine what cord and charger go with each gadget (an ongoing adventure for me), but they still faced difficulties, just as we do today. Lessons and life repeat themselves.

No matter what you are going through in life today be completely and entirely cognizant someone, somewhere in the universe is going through the same thing. That is why your family, no matter how they fit into your life, are valuable gifts. Make sure you cherish them; share how you feel about them and why they are precious to you.

Share stories, dreams, hopes, fears, joys, and be a good solid shoulder to cry on. You may be amazed at the connections that bond you. We are all in this thing called Life together. None of us is alone. As you wrangle through the DNA hurdles focus on the one true fact: You are not alone! There exists an entire community dealing with the same issues. Plus, most of us have a tribe surrounding us. They are trying to get a handle on what you are going through so they can be the best person for you. Keep helping them to understand and share your concerns.

The more you tell of your adventure the more you help others toward comprehension and hopefully to better understanding about these life-changing moments so many of us are tackling. Don't keep your story a secret. Don't be ashamed or run from the facts and the results. If it is not your thing to put yourself out there, then keep it close to the vest. Everyone handles these things in their own way, and it is vital for each of us to remember and respect one another's decisions.

I cherish all of my Zeta Sisters, Sisters in Life and the men I consider to be my Brothers-In-Arms. We may not have served on the battlefield together, but we have shared moments of baptism by fire, and they would never desert me. I hope they feel the same and consider me to be a true sister.

You Can Pretend

You got the news today
News that I existed
You argued that it wasn't true
But you know in your Heart it is.
The stories you are hearing hit too close to home
	and ring too true to deny.
Yet, you shut down
Closed yourself off
And then tainted others around you
Convincing them to do the same.
And for what reasons?
To protect yourself?
Fear of the Unknown?
Void of loving others?
You can Pretend I don't exist.
But I do
And I am not going away.
I am a person, a human being with feelings and hurts that
This Discovery of a family I Never Knew has aroused
It has created a fire in my belly to learn more and to seek
	those that are part of me
They belong in my life and their blood flows through my veins.
Your denial of me only stokes the fire more!
Driving me to Reality
Pushing me to meet others never allowed into my Life
Encouraging me to learn My Truth and to help others
	Learn Theirs
You Can Pretend
But Facts are Stubborn things, and they don't lie.
Keep Pretending
It Only makes me Stronger in my Quest and for that
"I Thank You"

This was the first blog post I wrote after the disastrous reaction from my half-sister and her friend. She pulled out all the stops and they were not good stops, I might add. Her biggest issue was denying that "her father" ever had an affair and adamant he did not know my mother. Well, how would she know that? She was not born and of course, I agreed with her, there was no affair. My mom and "our father" met one another while they were both single and working in Downtown Dallas.

I had to share that this post sparked a nasty response, too. It was the catalyst which pushed me forward (or should I say shoved me into the front of the line). Fighting for the rights of others has always been part of my make-up and personality. When I began experiencing these negative behaviors it was painful, but it also made me completely aware something needed to be done to educate and advocate. My desire is for every NPE (Not-Parent Expected) to be a household term and through acceptance and understanding of the term it will initiate healing.

ACT III

CHAPTER 22

Ghosting

"To Ghost or Not to Ghost." That is the question.

Along the journey in finding my family the term "ghosting" has been brought up many times and tons of NPEs experience it. Truthfully, I cannot ever recall "ghosting" someone. If I have and you are the person I, unknowingly, did this to: *I am sorry!* There are many things worse than "ghosting," but it ranks up there in the TOP 10 Shitty things to do to another person. (David Letterman can borrow my list).

Just because, as humans, we don't have the courage to face issues and discuss them in an adult manner, it should never give way to treating someone as though they never existed.

The term "GHOSTING" became mainstream in the past decade. It became popular due to online dating. The term is often used in reference to romantic relationships, but also is prevalent in scenarios where contact has ceased completely by friends and family. Kimberly Troung wrote the following about "ghosting" in Refinery29:

> Ghosting, the noun, and to ghost, the verb, have been added to the dictionary, and have been defined as 'the phenomenon of leaving a relationship of some kind by abruptly ending all contact with the other person, and especially electronic contact, like texts, emails, and chats.

Hey, if a word like this gets a place in the dictionary, then we know it has become a significant issue in our society: an issue that none of us should be proud of and we should each strive to be better communicators. It is a passive aggressive way of telling someone to "go jump in a lake."

The flip side, however, are people who are told the truth and have been communicated with about the relationship ending. Yet, they keep coming back for more and won't let up in their endeavors to pursue the person kind enough to communicate properly. There are times when someone is abusive, conducting illegal activities, or presenting toxic behavior and they leave no choice but to be ghosted. These kinds of circumstances call for an immediate "ghosting," and one should take the hint they have been given a strong heave ho and walk away.

So why do people "ghost?" Mainly? They don't want to face the truth and they are usually people who will avoid confrontation and tough discussions at all costs. While most of us think ghosting is more common in romantic relationships, it has become very mainstay in the platonic world, too. We may think "ghosting" is a new phenomenon, but it has actually been occurring for decades. People have been cutting off communication, not answering calls and abruptly walking away for years.

While the ghoster is running as fast as they can from the situation, they are leaving a trail of loss, hurt, and grief behind in their wake. In my case, a first cousin reached out to me, and we had a great interaction. Then suddenly the older of my newly found half-sisters started making calls to family members telling them not to speak to me.

This first cousin was the child to my only living immediate family member—my uncle. She was positive, loving, and my heart was overflowing with the chance to meet her and my uncle. As quickly as we connected, she cut off all contact due to this bullying from the half-sister. Since then, my uncle passed away, leaving me with a loss difficult to define. All I wanted was to hear stories about my biological father and to connect the pieces. Sadly, this was taken from me.

It is my pain and I own it, but this is one of the most hurtful things biological family members can do to those of us that are merely seeking the truth.

Psychology Degree Guide addresses the psychological reasons someone ghost another and problems that Ghosting can cause:

1. Ghosting Hurts

This is the easiest fact to consider. It just plain hurts because it denies the other person an understanding of what they did wrong. It denies the other person the opportunity for closure. Yes, there are times where the only answer is to walk away but giving a person the chance to fix their own issue is the kind thing to do.

2. Damaging Self-Worth

Someone can be the most confident person in the world, but Ghosting can damage the self-worth of even the strongest of humans. Everyone is worthy of an explanation, no matter how bad or weak the explanation.

3. Rejection

Ghosting is a form of rejection. No one can argue this point. Being rejected in this manner may bring out even worse behavior from the person you are ignoring. Think about this before you cut off all ties with no conversation. It can cause confusion and the person may feel the need to prove they are the person you want or need.

4. Opposite Intent

People react differently to this behavior. Being a victim to the silence could set off a negative energy and response in the person. Someone with outwardly or underlying aggressive tendencies may become even more so when disrespected in this manner. You may create a monster, lurker, or stalker by not having the courage to confront the situation head-on.

The positive take away of being ghosted is we are probably better off without these people who have chosen to manage or rather mismanage issues or relationships in this manner. Unless it is necessary for them to flee from someone for their own safety, they are likely creating a pattern of immaturity, cowardly actions, and presenting themselves as someone who cannot be trusted or respected. Possibly these ghosters are showing a reflection of their own issues and most of us have no desire to be a party to that—ever. With this being said, they have done us a favor by walking away. None of us need this in our lives. We deserve better.

It is a common place story to hear of a Not-Parent Expected to have met a parent, relative or even a potential relative and then to be completely ignored afterwards. (Remember Sonny from chapter 11). Many NPEs may already be dealing with abandonment issues, being rejected in this way can be traumatic and can possibly cause existing emotional struggles to surface.

The Ghoster and the Ghostee, Neither One Wins

Been Ghosted? Whether it be in the NPE, romantic, or platonic world it happens to each of us. Remember you are not a victim. You and only you can make this decision. People have problems and it can be extremely draining to be around them. If this silencing has happened to you for any reason recognize two things:

1. It might be you and you may need to take some time for introspection and flush out the problem on your own since you did not receive the chance for closure or

2. This person may not be a person you want in your life. They may bring an array of difficulties into your realm you do not need nor want.

We cannot control others. We can only control ourselves, our actions and how we respond to the situation. Handle ghosting with dignity.

What will change is Us.

We will learn our lessons with Grace.

Make adjustments with Integrity.

Walk away with Compassion.

Share positive energy with Love.

But most importantly—We will be Free!

CHAPTER 23

Letter From My Father in Heaven

Since we are talking about "ghosts" it seemed appropriate to include my dream letter from my deceased biological father. It is a figment of my imagination, and these are the words that have been percolating in my soul for years. If only I had the chance to meet him things may have been different or perhaps things may have remained exactly as they are today. Either way it is fine, but it is fun to create the scenario of a "what if."

I encourage you to play with your own letter to anyone you desire to share thoughts and feelings. Write it, publish it, put it in a drawer or throw it away. Whatever you decide to do is fine, but just do it. See if it helps to get it out on paper. It does not need to be pretty, flowery, or for anyone else but you. I find it helpful to get it out of my heart and let the mind do the rest. So here is my letter from a man who I wonder what he would have done "If He Only Knew?"

Dear Lezlee,

By the way, I love the way your name is spelled, Lezlee Shontae. Exactly what I would have expected out of your mother—Pure Sass! Earlier you mentioned your prayer was for your mom and I to be talking and for us to have your back (along with all your other sensational relatives up here). To put your mind at ease, yes, we have your back and yes, your mother and I have had plenty of conversations here in Heaven. Some good and some pretty darned heated, which is understandable considering the circumstances.

Can you imagine my surprise when I got here on August 13, 2000, and learned about you? I was already a little shaken about the whole leukemia thing, dying so suddenly and way too young. Then I get here and learned there is a daughter down on Earth I was never told about, and they had thirty-seven years to tell me about you! I was a little frustrated, to say the least.

On a positive note, I am glad you are aware of this disease being part of your medical history. Knowing it would never have been in your thoughts had you not known about me makes me sad. You have the right to this type of valuable information. The good news is now you can keep an eye out during future check-ups. They say I fought a valiant fight, but honestly, there was no option to "fight." It was already too late, but every human deserves the right to know their heritage and their background. We need the chance to prepare when something unexpectedly comes our way. That is just one of the greatest gifts these DNA tests provide. They offer insight into the past, present, and future, which is truly miraculous.

You deserve to have a long and fruitful life. It really threw me for a loop when I got sick. It was so out of the blue and I was not ready to leave. There was still so much to do. I want you to have a fighting chance against any enemies whether it be human or a disease. Plus, if I had known about you, I really would not have wanted to go until at least being able to meet in person.

My apologies for the behavior of my other daughters. Some of it may be my fault in the way I raised them, and some may be them just being protective of their mother. As far as your cousins are concerned, I need to think on that one because they have no reason to reject you (nor do my daughters as far as that is concerned). In time, you may learn way more than you want and decide you are better off not being a part of the circumstances you are learning about through your discovery.

The truth is I met your mother and had a relationship with her several years prior to meeting my wife, the mother of my other children. Never in a million years did I know you were a result of the relationship or that I was a part of your creation. The girls really have no reason to be threatened by you. For goodness' sake, it is not like you are after some inheritance: my wife got everything, and the girls will inherit anything remaining from her. From what I understand, you are a success all on your own and the last thing you need is money from a long-lost parent.

Isn't it ridiculous how people can get things so screwed up in their heads? You brought up the word delusional earlier and that is truly delusional. It is not to say I would not have provided for you. If I had a clue about your existence before I died, there is no doubt I would have taken care of you. Of course, it would have been very important and something I would have done. However, it is too late to worry about the past and something that will never happen. Forgive me for being unaware of my own flesh and blood living just down the road all this time.

By now I am sure you have learned about your two brothers who died early in life. Such a heartache, and to be honest, knowing about you may have eased some of the pain, but again we cannot change the past. We can only look to the future and what it holds. Your bravery in seeking your truth is astounding. As your father, I am extremely proud you are doing this.

As humans, we spend too much time worrying about the things with little importance or the things which will never come to fruition. Focusing on the here and now is what matters. All of us up here assure you that fighting over the trivial stuff or making things bigger than they are is a waste of time and energy. Yet, people continue to go to the negative and create mountains out of molehills when what they should be doing is embracing life and loving one another. We all know life is way, way, way too short for all the silly crap! Continue to embrace your DNA Surprise and I beg you to stay on your path of helping others.

As far as your mom goes, she is as beautiful as I remembered and know why I loved her way back then. She seems to have a pretty good connection with the Man Upstairs, but she is still in a bit of hot water over the entire deception and lying thing. She is working through it, and she has been given a bit of grace since she was such a strong believer and great mom. She still has some explaining to do up here, but rest assured she is doing fine. Believe it or not she is actually working out and exercising because she is free from perspiration in Heaven and her hair won't get messed up. I am sure that gives you a bit of a giggle.

Your Daddy Paul is a great man and we have become good friends. Your mom is squirming a bit over it, but oh well, what is one to do? We all get along and that is just the way it is up here and should be the way it is down there. You were lucky to have him as a dad and he is extremely proud of you.

I also thank your dad, Bill, for finally spilling the beans and telling you the truth you so richly deserved in all this mess. If I could turn back time and be able to do something differently, rest assured, I would have done so. My relief in all of this is your mom kept you and you have had an amazing life despite my not being there. Though I wish I had been around to watch you grow into the incredible woman you are today.

By now you also know I loved golf, and it is fabulous you married a golfer. We would have gotten along marvelously; I just feel it in my bones (or should I say Spirit). In Heaven they say we will feel no pain or sorrow, but I get a mulligan on this one. They are wrong because it does hurt, I do mourn, and it fills me with sadness that I never got to meet my eldest child and her husband. You find humor in things that others do not, you love fashion, and you have a quick wit, all traits of mine. Some things are environmental, and some are just in the genes. There is no mistaking your genes and where they come from. You are a mix of incredible people.

It is time for me to go. Good luck with the book, it is going to be a best seller. I just know it! But most importantly, you are going to help millions of people get through this tough situation. God put you where He needs you. Make us all proud and help as many people as possible there on Earth. You have been thrown a fast ball and you will hit it out of the park.

You have also been given a gift that can turn this undeserved heartache around for the good. You are putting into motion a wave of truth, transparency, and love that is greatly needed in this world of DNA discovery. So many people need it so **do not give up**. No matter what! We are all up here watching over you and we Fist Punch and High Five for your accomplishments every day!

You Go Girl!

Eternally,
Your Father

CHAPTER 24

It's a Grieving Process

Learning you are an NPE can initiate the stages of grieving. Why? Because it is loss of life as we knew it. If you are upset or grieving due to your discovery, know that it is a normal emotion and reaction.

Perhaps you feel like a part of you has died. Just as you would grieve over a lost loved one or a divorce, we all mourn differently. If you are unaware of the stages of grief, it is worth listing them here. Per www.usurnsonline.com the stages are as follows:

1. Denial and Shock

2. Pain and Guilt

3. Anger and Bargaining

4. Depression

5. The Upward Turn

6. Reconstruction and Working Through

7. Acceptance and Hope

Let's discuss these stages together and see if you relate.

Denial and Shock

The denial is not just about the NPE. The pain of denial caused by bio family members can be intense and painful. Even though we are prepared, Ready, Set, Go to move forward, we will not always encounter the loving open arms we anticipated or desired. Or perhaps you are in shock and unable to believe what you are seeing on your tree and in the cM numbers. It is a lie. It is impossible. Your mind is racing and probably in denial.

There must be a mistake in the DNA test. This is always a possibility, but usually the proof is right in front of our eyes. Members of the newly found family may also be in denial and shocked by the news. It is up to them how they perceive the situation. However, as an NPE we are looking at the facts straight in the face.

It takes time to comprehend that our life as we knew it has changed, evolved and in some cases completely dissolved. Give yourself permission to grieve. At times I seem to shift around the various stages of grief.

Pain and Guilt

Unadulterated pain will pursue your discovery. If it doesn't? Perfect! You are way ahead of the rest of us, and your healing will hopefully take less time and effort. The loss can feel unbearable, and the overwhelming guilt can envelope you when you fear you are burdening others.

Unresolved issues become apparent. It may or may not be possible to ascertain those issues. Most people are not forthcoming with stories and secrets occurring in the past causing the division of the family unit. This can leave the seeker in the dark about what has happened in the past or what is causing people to respond the way they do.

We all have regrets in life. Past chaos and conflicts are potential barriers to moving forward.

Letting them grow out of proportion or containing them is up to us. How we act and react is our daily challenge in anything we do in life. We can choose to complain about thorns on roses or be glad there are roses among thorns.

The pain initiated from the lies, deception and manipulation is natural. Pain often erodes into guilt. Pain can feel like being lost at sea with no connection to anything accept vast open waters with no land in sight. Talk about a sense of loss and loneliness.

Consider guilt. Guilt can be a heavy load to bear and cumbersome to carry and off load. Determining the source of the guilt is even more challenging, especially when you did not create the problem. Guilt is sense of regret or responsibility for thoughts, words, or actions. It comes along when you perceive you have harmed someone, made a mistake or gone against some moral code of conduct.

The determination of NPE status should bear no guilt on behalf of the NPE. Why should a person being merely the product of a situation, a relationship, a decision be held accountable for the suffering of others? There will be those holding the belief we are at fault for the situation. This is a total crock. These are decisions made way before you came along, and when you did appear, the decisions were made without any input from you.

Please do not let others guilt you into thinking you have no right to question and seek answers. Be gentle with yourself and others. It will make a world of difference. Toxic guilt does not belong to you, nor should you engage in the practice of carrying it around on your shoulders. It is not yours to keep.

Anger and Bargaining

Scream, Yell, Cry, Shout, Weep, Wail, Get Totally Hissy Fit Mad and then pull on your Big Girl/Boy panties/briefs and do something about it. Grief Therapist, Rabbi Brian of ROTB.org says, "Sit in the pain and discomfort."

Well, that doesn't sound like much fun. Here is the deal. You cannot keep paddling as fast as you can or run from the facts of the matter forever. You will exhaust yourself and everyone involved. Consider it like ocean waves. The waves ebb and flow, taking fragments and particles out to sea and bringing back moss, shells, and sometimes unwanted items. Yet, it is a natural on-going phenomenon. One that will not stop or give up.

There will be times the waves are so powerful you will be pulled under into the abyss of the unknown. It washes over you until you feel like you are drowning. Stop panicking and let the natural flow of the current bring you back to the top and breathe, gasp, suck in fresh air. It does not matter how you decide to survive. Just do it!

As far as bargaining goes, there have been many conversations with God about how to handle the whole thing. What do I do? What are my next steps? What did I do to deserve this? Lots of questions but in all honesty, I never bargain with God. He has this and as hard as it is I work hard at letting Him guide this ship. Oh, of course, I jump on the boat and steer it most days. Hey, I love being in control of my own destiny. He has an alternate plan every day, but you can't blame a girl for trying to navigate the rough waters all on her own.

Then comes the realization that I should hand the wheel back over, open my eyes and free myself from the emotions surrounding me. This is not a spectator sport, nor do I believe it can be managed alone. Your Crew will get you through.

Depression

Xanax hear me calling! Just kidding.

There may come a time when you need help dealing with the madness, and a good counselor or psychiatrist could be what you need. There is absolutely no shame in that. Get the help you need and deserve. I shared the story about one of the first responses on my blog, this woman telling me, "You need help, and you don't have the right to push your family members."

First, you're "damned skippy" I needed help, and I was getting it! Secondarily, she mentioned her adoptive situation and she never pushed anyone to discover her past. Well, as I have said, that is totally up to her and that each of us walks our own walk. She handled life the way she chose, but for me, it is not enough. Her nastiness drove me to setting another counseling appointment for the next day, and my counselor and I got a big belly laugh over the entire encounter.

How did she think I got to the point of posting, sharing, and writing the story? It was from getting help and making myself vulnerable in exposing my story. She provided another moment of truth, encouraging me to speak up and advocate. My mantra became "Ignorance is a true waste of Intelligence," and as the great comedian Ron White would say, "You can't fix stupid!"

People will be what they will be and all we can do is keep getting the word out and educating the masses about the NPE situation.

Isolation and seclusion are common in the DNA discovery whether it is held deep inside, or you are voyaging into uncharted territory where no man or woman has gone before. It is a sensory reaction to be reckoned with. Processing the plight you have undertaken can be all-consuming. Been there and done that.

Trying to explain what is going on inside and out seems like a futile task most days. Putting it into words is even more problematic. How can you explain what you don't understand and have never encountered?

Each time I share my story attendees ask me, "How did you feel?"

"Like Shit"

"Pissed as Hell"

"Madder than a Wet Hen" (by the way that is pretty upset here in the south).

I wanted to shout. That is exactly what people want to hear. Honestly for me, and I have shared this hundreds of times, I felt pure R-E-L-I-E-F! Finally, I had proof I was not delusional or crazy. (Well, the jury may still be out on that one.)

In the beginning, it felt like I was on an island all alone. My mistake, I was not. There were friends and family around and they loved me so much. I am so thankful for them. Though they may not have understood the situation, got confused when I tried to explain my new family tree and needed a whiteboard to follow along, they stuck with me. There are family and friends just shocked and baffled by the entire issue, yet they continue to support me. When the boat rocked, they steadied me; when I was drowning, they threw me a life jacket; and when I was in troubled waters, they rowed me to shore.

Never let pride get in the way of asking for help and telling your story. You will be amazed at how interesting it can be for others to hear about your experience. In the interim, you might assist in building a bridge for others in the same boat. It never fails when I tell my story everyone knows someone at some level of this situation.

The Upward Turn

I continue to waver between the stages of grief. At times, hurt reveals itself and tears unexpectedly flow. Other times anger springs forward with a wave of bitterness, frustration, and resentment over why no one ever trusted me with my own truth. Denial is long gone, so I have that one tackled, even if others in my genealogical making remain in this dismissal phase.

Bargaining? Maybe a little when I wish a chance to join my past, present, and future into one dinner table. You will join me for my imaginary dinner in an upcoming chapter. Inviting whomever I want and serving whatever I want gives me pleasure and peace. Even if it is only in my daydreams—it is still a miraculous healing tool.

Writing this book, sharing with others, and advocating for DNA surprises and discoveries is my Upward Turn. It took some time to weed out the garbage in my head and what I was being dealt. Life is about waiting and being patient. Admittedly, these are not my greatest attributes but this journey, late in life, has helped me realize my impact on others and that words do matter.

At times, a pause can bring purpose and enlightenment to us and others. What lies beneath the impatience and turmoil of the soul are gifts unimaginable. Breathing, praying, and meditation can all prove to be beneficial.

Reconstruction, Working Through It, Acceptance and Hope

These can formulate into one big package.

Acceptance is not validation you are okay with the circumstances. It merely means this is a new norm in your life. Realizing the world will never be the way it was is about planning the next steps. This is a necessary step in the healing process. Grasping the reality of the situation and understanding there is no turning back the clock can swaddle you in comfort. It is time to stop fighting the inevitable and cloak yourself in love and self-growth.

At this point, reconstruct your life into what you want or keep things status quo, just the way it has always been. There is no shame or problem with doing so. The thing to remember about grief is everyone experiences it and handles it differently. It is personal and each person's unique balancing act to behold and do with as desired.

These stages may come in different orders and at times blast the beholder with all seven stages at once. Yikes, what a day that will turn out to be. When it does happen keep someone on speed dial to bring over a bottle of wine and pizza with everything on it! Some people experience a few of these stages while others encounter and conquer each stage every single day. This is your grief—deal with it as you see fit but for goodness' sake deal with it!

Lastly, hold on to faith and hope it will all work out. We must put the work in, and addressing the issues at hand are the first steps. Like anything in our lives, if we keep sweeping hurt and shame under the rug the dirt piles up, and eventually, we are left with a big lump of garbage.

Do the heavy lifting of healing whether it be counseling, meditation, prayer, yoga, exercise or sharing your story with others. Healing via hope, faith, and honesty is available for the taking. Grab it with both hands, pull it tight to your body and your heart and mind can do the rest. Like anything, it takes work.

Lincoln Steffens, an American journalist and muckraker, shares a lesson he learned as a child. It relates to an artist painting a picture of muddy water. He told the artist he did not like the painting because there was too much mud in it. The artist concurred, yet pointed out the beauty he recognized in the contrast and colors of the river as the light played upon it and darkness drew near.

Will your story be about the mud or beauty of your discovery? When we find what we are looking for, we find what we seek in the stream of our life. Finding the beauty is much easier (and fun) than swimming in the muck.

Yuck!

The Grief You Hide

You are a rare and precious gem.

A person who has faced many struggles in life but remains kind, honest and strong.

What you see is what you get: no fakery, no sugar-coating, and no lies.

You have a heart of pure gold and a love that shines as bright as the sun.

You were betrayed in the past, but you have never let it turn your heart to cruelty.

You are a beacon of hope and faith and are consistently a pillar of strength for so many.

You bring warmth and joy to those around you.

Though carrying the pain of past losses, you continue to live life to the fullest.

Live that life with a smile on your face and love in your heart.

Raise your voice to the sky and dance to the beat of your own drum.

For no one will do it for you.

Only you can make it happen!

Author Unknown

CHAPTER 25

Double NPE-Carmen's Story

Carmen and I met at a Hiraeth, Hope & Healing Retreat in 2023. We became walking buddies, and her story intrigued me because not only did Carmen discover she was an NPE once, but she had a second discovery which makes her a Double NPE. Learning about all this one time is enough for most anyone, but to go through it twice is incomprehensible. It is uncommon for this to occur, but it does happen. Carmen and I both believe advocating and educating others about the NPE experience is the way to greater understanding and acceptance. This is just one reason I requested to tell her journey.

Here is her story:

> I was six years old when my mother, in a rage, disclosed to me the man who was raising me was not my father. She angrily shared that my father had died and to never look for the family because they wanted nothing to do with me. This was my first NPE experience, and I remember the tone in her voice as she spoke the harsh words. It left me feeling deeply sad and confused. I wondered what was wrong with me and why would my family not want to have anything to do with me.

> Eventually this led to feelings of unworthiness, low self-esteem, and low self-worth, something I have struggled with for years. Over

time my mother would tell stories about my father, and I would hang onto any details that seemed important. I often dreamt of meeting family one day and proving I deserved their love. It interested me that they were French Canadian, since I grew up in Canada, where both English and French are spoken.

My mother's family immigrated from Germany in 1953. Growing up I always proudly stated I was half German/half French Canadian. When I was twelve, I discovered a death certificate with information contradictory to the stories my mother had been telling. Noting the date of death, I tucked this key piece of information away. In 1995, at the age of eighteen I became pregnant and began longing deeply to find my father's family. This was half of my identity and also a part of my unborn child's identity. I took the information from the death certificate, went to the local library, and looked up my father's obituary on microfilm. I found the names of his brothers and decided to start there, as their last names would remain unchanged in marriage. Using the local telephone book, I found them both listed. I cannot tell you how many times I partially dialed the number and hung up. All I could hear was my mother's voice saying, "Don't bother looking for the family, they want nothing to do with you!"

After numerous attempts I finally let it ring. The voice on the other end said, "Hello." I replied with a shakiness in my voice. "My name is Carmen, and I am your brother's daughter."

From there I was welcomed into the family with open arms and spent the next twenty-six years reconnecting with family. They had actually tried looking for me at times, but to no avail. The past was history, and we could not change what had happened. The stories I was told did not matter. We just focused on the future. Little did I know what the future had in store and how relevant the pieces of those stories would become.

In March of 2021, I decided to take a 23andMe test for health reasons. On May 21, 2021, I woke to an email that said congratulations you're 50 percent Italian. This one statement from a test merely taken for health reasons sent my heart into my stomach and my head into a spiral. Trying to wrap my head around the results took a few months. It took a couple more DNA tests for me to truly accept my new reality: my new identity.

Once I was finally able to accept it all, I discovered the term NPE. Even though I knew an unfamiliar road lay ahead, familiar feelings returned. These feelings led to the realization all this felt strangely familiar because I had been here before through the lens of a child, and now, I was experiencing those same feelings as an adult. I was not just an NPE, but I was a Double NPE. My emotional response felt like déjà vu because I was reliving the same emotions. This gutted me and brought me straight back to the six-year-old whose life was turned upside down. Except this time, I learned my true cultural identity but nothing about my true biological father. I have spent a lifetime grieving a dead dad, and now I could have a dad that is still alive!

As a Double NPE this experience is deep-rooted to the core of who I am as an individual. My inquisitive nature, resilience, and drive keep me going forward in seeking answers and truth. As I continue this journey a large part of my healing process is engaging within the NPE community. Hearing other people's stories and wanting to share my own is healing and it happens within community. I also hope to bring awareness and education to others outside the community because this experience is more common than most people realize. No matter how you find out, whether someone personally drops the identity bomb, or you spit into a tube and a test result reveals one or both of your parents is not your biological parent, your life is forever changed.

CHAPTER 26

Guess Who's Coming to Dinner?

Have you ever watched the famous movie with Sidney Portier *Guess Who Is Coming to Dinner*? It is a classic and presents a surprise guest. A Black man at a White person's dinner table back in the sixties: you can't be any more controversial than that!

Plenty of controversy surrounds the DNA discoveries, surprises, and craziness of today. So, I could not help but throw a little bit of a historical film into the mix. In these times of inclusion, diversity, and acceptance it is a must-see movie. By the way, this is the topic for my next book *Color Blind*. I was taught to never see the color of the skin but to see the person, the real person, and never judge anyone due to their color. Today that has changed trajectory and I am forced to know if someone is "of color," pressed to know that this business or that business is black-owned, female-owned, etc. but that is for another day.

Let me progress rather than digress.

All the rage these days is the game Our Dinner List—Who Would be at Your Dinner Party?

So, I decided in true fad fashion to create and share my own "Guess Who's Coming to Dinner" list.

Hope you enjoy this diversion. I think you will recognize the actors.

Who would you invite and why?

Who you invite to a party can make or break the entire ambiance. The best parties are those filled with people of different mindsets, backgrounds, and interests. No problem making that happen. I will stick with the main characters in the play, some alive and some deceased. Mom, Don (BF), Paul (SF), Bill (BCF), Dick Reynolds (great uncle who wrote "Silver Threads and Golden Needles." I never met him), Anne Wojcicki (co-founder of 23andMe), Ellen DeGeneres (because she is always inclusive and would be a great moderator and add some humor to a touchy situation), Melissa Peterman (the actress because I adore her and think she can make any party a good time and help the conversation flow). If I could include all my gal pals it would be great, but this time, we will keep it small and intimate.

What would you discuss?

Well, duh! Of course, how, when, and where this NPE thing happened? Yes, I want the gory details. I want to verify if Don ever knew or had any indication of my existence.

Now that mom is gone there is no reason for embarrassment, so I definitely want to know why she did not come clean when the writing was on the wall. She knew I had discovered the truth, so why did she not discuss it and clear the air? Angels can only tell the truth and are not allowed to get mad, so this would be a win-win across the board.

Anne would be there to verify these findings are a common occurrence, and it is Okay.

What would you serve?

Cocktails First: Champagne is a must! So, lots and lots of Mumm, Moet, or Veuve Clicquot.

Martinis with Indigo Gin: It has that uncomplicated but oh so distinct strawberry infusion.

Need to be careful because I really don't want a romantic ambiance. Not sure if ghost or spirits can get sexy, but there is no way we are going to take that chance. It is what got us here in the first place.

On the Menu?

Brie with baguette to start.

Escargot—Guests would probably prefer to eat snail rather than crow.

Dinner is going to be Meat, Meat,and more Meat! What? Why not?

They are all already dead, or if living they can handle one night of meat. Comfort food full of love, hearty, and uncomplicated. No one is allowed to be on a diet for this night. If Anne, Melissa, or Ellen are vegans, we will have to make some arrangements, no biggie.

Terry Lee's venison, Mag's ribs, Jeff Bojeski's brisket are on the menu. The men in my living world have an immense talent with meat . . . in a good way.

Side salad (I mean, they still need their greens) and some yummy scalloped potatoes.

Though I love to cook I am going to be too nervous to make anything so leaning on friends is a must for this endeavor.

Daou Cabernet Sauvignon to pair with the amazing meats.

What music is playing?

No party is complete without the perfect playlist. The best way is to include music from different genres and generations. Starting slowly and then getting a little sassier as the night moves on.

This is the well thought out playlist created for this special night.

Allan Sherman—"Hello Muddah, Hello Fadduh"

Marvin Gaye—"Sitting on the Dock of the Bay"

Herb Albert and The Tijuana Brass—"Tangerine." My brother tells me Mom played this when we were little so I thought it might jog some memories. Might be playing with fire, but it's my party and I am dealing the cards as I see fit.

UB40—"Red, Red Wine" (has always been one of my favorites)

Tom Jones—"Sexbomb," "What's New Pussycat?," "I Love You." Mom was crazy about Tom Jones just like every other hot-blooded woman during the sixties and seventies. Now this man could shake it and woo the girls with his lyrics and tight pants.

Van Morrison—"Have I Told You Lately That I Love You." I need to pull down the sexy atmosphere from Mr. Jones, plus this was mine and Mag's wedding song.

Meagan Trainor—"Dance Like Your Daddy." I have always loved to dance and, if I must say so myself, I'm pretty good at it. I want to see if my bio daddy can actually dance. Maybe it is where I got it. Not sure Mom ever really shook her groove thang much so surely it came from somewhere.

Chubby Checker—"Let's Do the Twist"

Dolly Parton, Tammy Wynette and Emmylou Harris and Loretta Lynn along with Linda Ronstadt—"Silver Threads and Golden Needles." Playing tribute to my uncle and the proud ownership I have in this song.

Bette Midler—"Wind Beneath My Wings." This was my mom and Paul's song.

Mariah Carey—"Never Forget You." When it is finally time to wrap up the evening there will be hugs and tears. I will hold these memories forever and be so glad I had the opportunity to gather these amazing people in one place, so Mariah takes us home.

What is the Vibe?

Groovy, vintage, vibe of the sixties. What does that look like? It is a passion of mine to create tablescapes and themed parties so I will be going all out on this vibe. Using 33rpm LP vinyl records as chargers with red dishes and 45rpm singles hanging from the chandelier. Everyone is required to wear flower power and polyester outfits. Men need to wear buzzcuts. One relative shared that my bio dad wore a buzzcut well into later life, so this will be perfect. The chicks need to figure out a good old fashioned beehive doo. Lots of flowers and bright colors.

When do you know the party was a success?

1. I finally got straight answers to my questions.

2. Everyone exchanges Heavenly Emails, Texts, TikTok pages, Instagram pics. We will be able to see the spirits of various family members on this particular evening. So, as we end the evening, they will materialize and hugs all around before everyone heads back to their celestial worlds on Earth and in heaven. Amen!

Let's do this!

BON APPETIT!

Room at the Table

Sit down beside me
There is plenty of room
Take a minute to know me
And I will do the same for you
For there is room at the table for all of us
To share our hurts, our love, and stories of survival
No judging allowed
For there is too much of that going around
Let's break bread and learn from each other
About inclusion and acceptance
For there is far too little of that these days
Look at me. Really look at me
You may like what you see
But without an open heart
You will never know the depths of my soul
And I must say, I am someone you truly want to know
Give it a chance
Stop avoiding the truths and living in denial
There is plenty of room at my table
It is full of love, life, and laughter
No hatred or discrimination accepted
Now take a seat and lean in very close
I have something to tell you
You are safe here
Whatever your fears
They are unwarranted and unnecessary
Let them go far, far away
And enjoy your Room at the Table

CHAPTER 27

Genetic Mirrors

Many people are familiar with the term "genetic mirrors." It is primarily associated with adoption. Most people are not aware of this term and its meaning outside of the adoption world. When a person grows up with blood relatives and they share DNA, the genetic mirroring exists all their life but they are just not aware.

We all have heard the comments when a baby is born of which parent the child looks like or they have their Daddy's eyes and Mommy's smile. When people tell a child they are just like their mom because she is artistic, or a son or daughter are compared to grandparents that were great athletes they gain a form of genetic mirroring and belonging. These are usually comments and comparisons making a person feel proud, validated, and included.

So, what is genetic mirroring? It is the ability to see oneself in the family surrounding them due to their shared DNA, providing a basis of similarities to their culture, racial, and ethnic roots. It can create a roadmap of sorts to our identity.

Most people have great pride in their roots and where they obtained certain traits. Of course, there are many who would rather run from these facts than acknowledge their likeness in someone else. When it is pointed out that we look like or act like another person, it creates a bond and reinforces connections between people. It is a way of acceptance and the realization that people belong together.

Often, we may not want to share a certain trait, like when someone is quick to anger or they are a "Debbie Downer." Recognizing these traits can be helpful in making sure we don't go down that path in life and welcome the fact we can change the trajectory of our behavior.

With all of this said, you can see where this is more highly understood in the adoption world because adoptees usually do not have access to genetic mirrors. It can mold and impact the adoptee's identity.

Now the question is, "Lezlee why does this affect you? You are not adopted."

It is my opinion and belief that a DNA surprise can trigger genetic mirroring and can affect anyone with a Not-Parent Expected event. This is true whether a person finds a biological parent they were unaware of, someone is learning they were a donor conception, there was a medical error, they were a result of non-consensual sex, or in certain cases they were kidnapped at birth. All these circumstances can create a Not-Parent Expected event. We begin looking for like-nesses in the family we meet.

One of the reasons I never questioned my parentage is due to look-ing exactly like my mother. There was no doubt who my mother was and therefore, since I was told who my biological father was, there was no reason to question. I have piercing blue eyes just like my birth certificate father, my brother looks just like him, and my brother was my brother. Why would I have any doubts?

Remember at the beginning of this book it was never my intent to seek answers somewhere else. There existed a strong belief of belong-ing. My grandparents on both sides always provided connections so there was always a sense of being part of the pack.

But the comments, "If you only knew" and "If you knew what your mother did you would not believe it. You would be so upset with her."

are what drove me to the "crazy point" of curiosity. It became a thorn in my side and a strong driver toward the truth.

Genetic mirroring starts early in life. Have you ever looked in the mirror and wondered where your eyes came from? Or who has red hair? Long legs? The list goes on and on as we compare ourselves to the people around us. Throughout my life my nose was my varying factor. It did not resemble anyone in my family. Everyone had aquiline type noses, also called a Roman nose, and it gives the appearance of being curved or slightly bent. The aquiline nose was deemed a distinctive feature of Native American tribes.

This made sense to me. According to the tales my great-great-grandmother was a full blood Indian named Rebecca Featherhead (or something like that). We looked for these genetic characteristics in each other. I was told this was where I got the dark, thick, straight hair and why my mom and I could step out into the sun and instantly tan.

Like thousands of other DNA testers, we were all shocked and amazed that we had zero, absolutely zero, American Indian in our results. I think my mom took it the hardest. This was a level of pride and honor for her, and it was taken away in an instant. To add insult to injury, she thought she had named me after a maiden Indian name from a movie she watched. However, when she finally delivered me, I was tipping the scales at over eleven pounds, and she had gained seventy-five pounds. She was not a big woman, so this was a massive undertaking, and all thoughts of names and spelling went out the door with the delight of her finally giving birth.

In the beginning of these testing shenanigans, I was not looking for these differences in taking the Ancestry.com test. Yet, when I was up to bat again with the 23andMe test, it was vital for me to get those variances. It was the moment of truth that had been gnawing at me for years. My stomach sank when I saw "half-sibling" but at the same time tears of joy and relief emerged with the gratification that I was not crazy, delusional, or believing a whim.

Voila!

There it was on the computer screen. A family tree with new branches, leaves, and contacts.

This by no means was the final answer! This was just the beginning of many twists and turns to follow, but at least at that moment there was a starting point. So, for me the two words "genetic mirroring" reversed and now I call it "mirroring genetics." Why? Because I started looking in the mirror and began working out my genetics. For me all of this did not change the person I was but not everyone feels this way.

This newfound knowledge can shake many people to their core. Please don't get me wrong. The struggle is real, tears can appear over the smallest of things, and I can get choked up by just telling a portion of my story to a complete stranger. No way am I immune to the devastation that can come with the shock. Yet, I love seeing myself in new family members.

Pictures are truly worth a thousand words, and I am blessed to have been gifted with some pictures of family members. The greatest thing about photos given to me is that I finally found my nose!

It is paramount that genetic mirroring or, my new term mirroring genetics, be addressed. Acknowledging genetic mirroring is a big deal in the development of a person's identity, personality, and behavior as a first step. Adoptees should be encouraged to seek out genetic mirroring for their evolution and growth. No matter the status of each individual, whether they are adopted or learning they have a different DNA makeup, they should be permitted to question.

These discoveries can create sadness, anxiety, loneliness, and feelings of isolation. Hopefully, with further understanding we can shift those feelings to joy, happiness, gratification and belonging.

Now go look in the mirror and put your lipstick on or shave your face. Love yourself for all that you are. Recognize your authentic self and become more comfortable with the uniquely beautiful or extraordinarily handsome face that stares back at you. We all have flaws. This growth of self-acceptance can be slow and subtle, especially when we have been looking at a slightly different person all these years.

I am the same person inside and outside, but now it seems I linger just a little bit longer looking in the mirror. The features of my ancestors remain, but my nose takes on an entirely different meaning. The eyes staring back at me are slightly confused and a bit disoriented. It is a good thing, and I am no longer fearful of what I might find when asking questions or trying to learn the truth.

The ultimate truth is these discoveries can cause discomfort and uncertainty. In my humble opinion and through experience, embracing these revelations is the way to mitigate the pain.

Once I told someone who was being extremely rude about our DNA connection, "Being ignorant is a waste of your intelligence."

Interestingly, this offended them. This was not an insult. In fact, it was a compliment to them for being intelligent. So why would she waste those smarts on staying in the dark on the subject? It was obvious that was someone wanting to avoid the facts and ignore the truth. If it has not been mentioned before: Move on from these folks! Life is too precious and short to hang with negative, energy-zapping people.

Maybe the old saying, "Ignorance is bliss" is where some people need to land. This is everyone's personal choice, but it is our choice of how we act or react to the toxins surrounding certain people. I say get up and walk on (or flat-out sprint) away from these folks as quickly as possible. If you are one of these people, it is my prayer you are learning from this book, and you will continue on your own journey of discovery to kindness and acceptance. This roller coaster you are riding is tough, and healing is vital for you, too.

Face

Face the Facts-no matter how difficult.

Face your accusers, doubters, and antagonists. Look them in the Face and say, "No More!"

No more will you Slap me in the Face with your cruelty.

Put on a Poker Face when you go into negotiate.

Put on a Straight Face when you want to laugh out loud but really shouldn't.

Be thankful you don't have to wear a Face Mask anymore.

Want a Face Lift?   Get One! Need a New Face Cream?   Buy It!

Miss Your Grandkids?   Facetime Them!

Face the mirror and really look at the beauty in your eyes, the slant of your perfect nose, the shape of your sensual lips. Face It this is who you are. Perfect in every way.

Now make a Face, a funny face, pouty face, scary face. Any face will do.

Go Face-to-Face (or toe-to-toe) with a difficult situation that must be faced.

And when you have Fallen on your Face pick yourself up and brush off the dust.

Recognize you can talk and talk until you are Blue in the Face and nothing is going to change.

Now Face the Music, get out of your way and Dance Like Nobody is Watching.

Remember on the Face of Things it may look grim, but Face It, every cloud has a silver lining.

If you committed to going to a party, event, or special occasion, be sure to Show Face.

Save Face and stand with Integrity.

Face your demons, Face your dragons, and naysayers.

Once you get a good look, resist the temptation to do an immediate About-Face.

Release the Warrior in you, put on Face Paint, and Face the World.

CHAPTER 28

All Roots Lead to Comanche (and Brownwood, Texas)

There are times when I feel like I am living a real-life *Mama Mia* Moment. However, I am not on some beautiful Greek Island, but rather I landed in the quiet and inviting town of Comanche, Texas.

Comanche is a seemingly sleepy little town, but I beg to differ. It is a hotbed of family members on my personal trail of tears. So, I have found an affection and love for a town never before on my radar. Comanche, population of approximately 4,300, is the county seat of Comanche County. In 1950, there was a stronger population than exists today, but that is understandable with modernization and migration into larger towns.

It was established in 1858 by John Duncan when he offered the county 240 acres on Indian Creek. A military road known as the "Corn Trail" came through in 1850 to supply area forts and encourage settlement. The town was established in 1856, and the city was incorporated in 1858. Near the modern courthouse is the preserved log structure known as the "Old Cora Courthouse," one of the oldest standing wooden courthouses in Texas. Cora, the former county seat, later became Gustine.

As I have learned more about my heritage all roots lead to Comanche, with many family members in nearby Brownwood and Abilene. My new friends, Pamela Hance, Eddie Cox, and Vickie Gore Harvick have been amazing in helping me unearth many answers to questions I had not even thought to ask. These guys were complete strangers but took me under their wings and guided me further into my lineage. In fact, this genealogical gang determined another potential side of my family within the Gore family tree, more relatives connecting me even stronger to Comanche.

Discovering your origins can be a magical moment. It has been for me. Finding ancestors, celebrating family ties, and embracing your culture can open your eyes to an entirely new perception of life. It has also proven to boost self-image and an individual's uniqueness.

Whether it is earlier in life or a later life realization, knowing your history and roots is a true advantage. How you perceive and handle it is up to you. You can run and hide or embrace the inevitable. Knowing can help you to appreciate different cultures perhaps you never understood.

Newfound knowledge is amazing and can strengthen your understanding of others and expand your horizons. I love it and have chosen to become a part of Comanche as much as possible. I never thought after six decades of life my world would explode. Just like a firework display there are colors across the spectrum. There are moments when you *oooohhhh* and *aahhhh*, and there are times you are left disappointed and wanting for more. There are always the complete duds in the package. These are the ones you must be careful with, because they can ignite at any given moment and cause serious damage with no warning.

Something I read recently addressed people changing their names to their newfound sur names. I am positive I will not do this because I already have too many names in the mix: Ballard (BCN),

Martin (SFN), Haight (First Marriage), Liljenberg (Married Name), Carver (BFN). It is a lot to absorb and so many aliases the government is going to start questioning me about citizenship.

In addition to Comanche, Brownwood and Abilene, Texas also became part of the picture because immediate family members had migrated to these areas as they married, raised children, and started businesses. It is a point of pride, as I now know my heritage includes a long line of entrepreneurs and God-loving people. Faith, hope, and love run through my veins on all sides of my upbringing and my unknown family. No bank robbers or hooligans, yet. But hey, I say, "Bring it on!" The more the merrier in this insane balancing act between past, present, and future. All these factors shape us into what we were and will be.

Comanche is a part of me. I recently joined the Comanche Chamber of Commerce, and have visited stores, restaurants, and hotels there. Every detail, and every person I meet makes an indelible mark on me. I will make sure I am a part of Comanche and the people that live there for as long as possible. My latest purchase was a t-shirt in bright red stating, "You Can Take the Girl Out of Comanche, but You Can't take Comanche Out of the Girl." How apropos is that? I am embracing my newfound community—it just feels right!

We have lost pride in our roots, and we need to get it back. It does not matter if you came from a little town in rural Anywhere that no one knows about or if you are from a major metropolitan area. Own your roots and your past. They belong only to you. You can decide to be embarrassed, ignore it, or make sure the entire world knows you are a magnificent and remarkable person that came from _____ (fill in the blank). Make the place you came from proud and let them hear your voice whether you are close by or thousands of miles away.

Could it have been more fun to find my roots in Santorini? Well Sure! But it is a long way to travel to discover new territory and to explore the past, so I am delighted I can jump in the car, drive two hours, and be with open-minded people, some family, and some newly found friends. Comanche and Brownwood are communities providing open arms, information galore, and a love I was unable to find from the folks I have already mentioned several times ad nauseum. As I edited this book over and over it has become obvious that I am still a bit bitter. Hey, this is continual work to get past this stuff some days.

It is a shame to see all the people who are unable to embrace the unknowns and choose to live in a world of misunderstanding and ignorance. As an NPE you will encounter all of it. Be prepared for the inevitable, protect your heart and soul, but do not let these nay-sayers keep you down. There is an entire community cheering you and every seeker on to the success of learning the past. They have no fear when it comes to holding you tight and wiping away your tears of pain and those of joy.

CHAPTER 29

Road Less Traveled

My favorite poem has always been "The Road Less Traveled" by Robert Frost.

> Two roads diverged in a yellow wood,
> And sorry I could not travel both
> And be one traveler, long I stood
> And looked down one as far as I could
> To where it bent in the undergrowth;
> Then took the other, as just as fair,
> And having perhaps the better claim,
> Because it was grassy and wanted wear;
> Though as for that the passing there
> Had worn them really about the same,
> And both that morning equally lay
> In leaves no step had trodden black.
> Oh, I kept the first for another day!
> Yet knowing how way leads on to way,
> I doubted if I should ever come back.
> I shall be telling this with a sigh
> Somewhere ages and ages hence:
> Two roads diverged in a wood, and I—
> I took the one less traveled by,
> And that has made all the difference.

This poem speaks to me. It reiterates the point that taking a difficult path is fine and it will make all the difference in our lives. It is Okay to be nervous and afraid of the course in front of us, but we have choices. There will be times we take the easier route and there will be occasions we decide the uphill battle will be worth the effort.

Any decision is just fine. We possess freedom and can always change our minds.

Whether this is your personal DNA Journey, or you are supporting someone searching for the answers there are a few certainties you will encounter.

1. There will be Naysayers.

As already stated, do not listen to them! Confronting the demons and dealing with the circumstances is the way to healing. This is a trauma to the NPE.

2. People will not understand the path you have chosen.

Everyone's path in life is different, and we each must chose what is best for our individual health and sanity. The people who love you should understand where you are coming from and stand by you in where you are going. Everyone handles the DNA surprise and discoveries differently.

I am not a psychologist and nor do I need to be to recognize and know we are each unique. We love, grieve, learn, absorb, and embrace differently. Thank God for the differences, because it would be a very boring world if we were all alike. There have been too many times to count when I was discouraged and wanted to stop this insanity and this search. How did I feel about that? Frustrated! Why in the world would anyone tell me it is not my right to understand and recognize my own life and how I was created? This will always be part of the discovery package. I get it. I don't like it, but I will dance around it and in the long run it is still my dance to dance.

3. Strangers will tell you what you should do and how you should do it even though they don't have a clue about your circumstances.

Until they are walking in your shoes there is not much to say. The truth of the matter is "you own this journey." It is yours and only yours, and we each must deal with everything on our own terms, not what someone else thinks. In the beginning, I had an attitude that we remain the same person and this newly found information did not change the person we have become.

This belief has shifted through experience. These events change all of us, and it does not have to be negative nor is it all going to be positive. In the past, it would have taken a tough day at the office or a sad event to make me cry or meltdown. Since discovering more and more about my individual circumstances, I can tear up in the strangest of situations. And "no" it is not menopause or hormones. Some days it is an emptiness that sets heavy on my heart. At times it is anger, and then the anger turns into survival mode where my mind begins focusing on combating danger. The danger? Losing people one-at-a-time as they age, and never getting the chance to meet them. With their loss goes another person who can share the story about my biological father and others in my biological sphere. The yarn of my life unravels with each passing moment. **Memory is a powerful tool, and the people I am losing are my only conduit to the truth.**

Here is an excerpt by Levi Davis in 2016 in referring to the symbolism of yarn in the game "Unravel." The article is titled "Unravel: A Spool of Memories and Symbolism." It perfectly creates an image releasing the fear of losing those that can share the stories:

Thoughts about our past govern how we live our lives and make choices in the future. They start off strong, freshly formed, and they fade behind us as we grow older and wiser. Memories connect us to who we are, who we were, and to the people and places that weave in *and out of our lives. Memory is a powerful device; it can sell things, conjure up emotion, and even rule the way someone lives his or her life. It can attach us to places, objects, and people we never thought possible, but above all else, memories can disappear completely.**

That is amazing and powerful!

I crave those memories and stories. It is something in my soul and spirit that is unexplainable.

There are days I compartmentalize and will not think about what has happened at all and focus only on family, friends, and work. Yet, there is always the underlying itch to get back into the DNA game and learn more, to reach out to another unknown family member. These are my experiences, and they are sometimes scary and at other times enlightening.

Will we cry? Yes.

Will we stomp our feet and lay down on the ground and throw a tantrum? You bet!

Is this acceptable? Absolutely!

There is no one, and I mean unequivocally **no one**, that can tell you how to feel and act. They will try. Yes, there is a level of grace and kindness that should be utilized, but that is part of everyday living. Being the person coming in with "both guns loaded" is not the answer, yet, at times it takes persistence and a thick skin to move to the next stage.

This journey is not easy, but I'm pretty sure you have picked up on that by now. Stay strong in your desire to learn more or to walk away from it all. There is no right or wrong.

Remember the first blog comment I mentioned earlier? The

---

* Levi Davis, "Unravel: A Spool of Memories and Symbolism," Disgruntled Dragon. Fan Clubs, February 24, 2016, https://www.fanclubs.org/articles/gaming/unravel-spool-memories-symbolism/.

response given to her was positive and loving. Her circumstances are totally different from mine. Does she really have the right to shame me and tell me I need to "let it go" and imply I have issues and need counseling? Probably not, but the fact of the matter remains, I am the one that started this. The one putting my story out there for all to read. Dealing with the negatives builds strength and fortitude for the message. If anything, those types of comments are a foundation more now than ever. They stress the need for the NPE stories to come to light.

I love counseling by the way so telling me I "need" counseling was like "cha-ching" and helped me know I was definitely on the right path. When I read this comment, I shouted out loud, "Darn right I do! Now what ya got?"

If it was intended to insult, it failed because this type of ridicule proves even more there are people out there without a clue as to what this NPE looks like. There are many people struggling with discovering their biological families whether it be through adoption, artificial insemination, or secrets kept and they need help and tolerance from others. Society can learn from all of this and rather than being afraid of the unknown it is possible to embrace the opportunities that are unfolding before us.

Isn't it funny that others are more afraid of the truth than the NPE? Let that soak in a minute. NPEs live the lies every day. We cannot run away. It is part of us day in and day out. Yet, the folks who have known their own truths throughout the years will often shun and dismiss the NPE. Of course, their feelings of confusion and anger are important and should not be dismissed. They must be acknowledged and respected. They did not ask for this either, but I stand my ground on the fact that:

We are the product of the circumstances.

We did not cause it.

Most of us have been living in the dark against our will, and

We are not a "Dirty Little Secret!"

Be true to yourself, and wherever this path is leading you, follow it. This is a path most will never have to venture. It is a path less traveled by the majority of the population even though there are more and more of us on this road together every day. The NPE population is growing and in a time of acceptance, inclusion, and diversification we are the new minority. This minority of people includes all races, genders, sexual orientations. You name it, and we are there! Just as with any minority we are an abnormality to those around us.

Time will tell where this is heading. I encourage everyone to jump on the NPE train and enjoy the ride. You have no idea where it will take you.

Always remember that if you go one direction you can always change your mind, back track, and take the path that is worn and holds comfort and different answers. Best of luck and love as you unravel your secrets. Hopefully, by doing so, you will never have to be subjected to comments like "If You Only Knew" because you will know the truth—Your Truth!

A Little Something Extra

In honor of National NPE Month (June), I developed the following list of fun things to celebrate this joyous occasion.

Top 10 Fun Things to do to Celebrate National NPE Month

1. Call or message someone on your Family Tree that you have not contacted.

2. Be Your Own Hallmark! Design your own NPE card (or just use blank cardstock) and send cards to another NPE to brighten their day.

3. Write a Top 10 List of the Blessings of Being (or Discovering) you are an NPE!

4. Post about being a NPE on your Facebook (or any social media).

5. Buy a Cupcake and a Candle for National NPE Month. Make a wish for yourself and all the other NPEs out there in the world.

6. If you were never able to meet your Birth Parent, write them a letter that you may not or cannot ever send. Do it for YOU!

7. Reach out to another NPE near you and invite them for coffee or a glass of wine. Share your stories.

8. Call a friend or family member that has been on this journey and tell them "Thank You" for their love & support.

9. Ask a question that you have been reluctant in asking a friend, family member or a stranger about your past.

10. Buy a book (just like this one) and gift it to someone on a DNA journey.

Acknowledgments

Where do I start? There are so many people to thank throughout this DNA surprise, search, journey, and discovery.

Magnus, you are the most amazing husband, confidante, and friend. This would never have become a reality had it not been for your love, support, and open mind.

Todd, my brother, your pushing me forward to take a second DNA test opened so many doors I had never imagined were possible. When we were young, we were partners in crime and as adults we circled back around and did it again.

Laura Weiss, my dear friend of over four decades. The best birthday present in 2021 you could ever give me was your fantastic research skills and finding my biological father's obituary. You have been through all of this with me from the beginning, never wavering or questioning. You have always given me encouragement to not give up and stay on track.

Dad, since the moment I was born you loved me no matter the circumstance. This was a hard secret to keep throughout these years and you never once faltered in being the best father. This has not been easy on you and no matter what has happened I will always be your daughter. There is nothing in the world that can change the truth.

To my amazing Sisterhood, all my gal pals and sorority sisters, thank you. Surely there have been times you thought I was a bit crazy (well, we know that is partially true), and yet you have stuck by my side, attending my events, and launch parties and encircling me with the reinforcements necessary to write this story.

ACKNOWLEDGMENTS

To my beta readers, Rebecca, Erin, and Ellen, your time and input were invaluable, and the NPEs that shared their stories, Lorna, Annie, Frank, and Carmen, thanks to each of you for putting yourself out there and sharing so others can learn from you.

Comanche, Texas. All roots led to Comanche where not only did I learn of family members from the Carvers to the Gores, but I found a unity in friends I never expected or anticipated. Every person I have encountered has opened their arms to me and each idea has been welcomed with open arms. Pamela, Eddie, Vickie, Nancy, Lydia, Wylie, Carver, Abby, Creek, and Gore family members, Micah, Kristy, Ann, Sharla, Sloan, Virginia, Kristy, Becca . . . the list goes on and on. This is just the tip of the iceberg of amazing people helping as we go to publication. Roots are very deep for me and learning they led me to Comanche, Texas is a true blessing.

NPEs of the World, I hope I can do you justice with this book. First, I hope it helps you in your journey and gives you hope, peace, and information to assist you along the way and into the future. Secondly, in being an advocate for NPEs, I pray that as people read this, they will see the different sides and facets of this phenomenon created through DNA testing. The NPEs I have met so far have changed my life, and someone once asked me, "What is your goal?". At first, I took offense to this, but no longer does this bother me. My goal? To help others navigate through "DNA Surprises and The NPE World" whether they are an NPE, someone holding the hand of an NPE or a person balking at accepting an NPE into their fold.

Mom, you gave me the best life anyone could ever ask for and you sacrificed so much for me. I have always understood why you did what you did and, there is no judgement. In retrospect, it happened exactly as it was supposed to because if it had happened any other way, I am sure I would never have written this book or picked up the challenge to help others in their discovery.

It is a precious gift.

Lastly, as a believer in Christ, there have been many days that have taken me to my knees. There have been tears of pain and of joy. The things other humans can do to us is indescribable, yet God places the saints among us to turn the grief into possibilities. While He is at it, He wipes the tears away. None of this would be possible without Him picking me up, dusting me off, and sending me down the path He chose for me in this endeavor. Amen!

Helpful Resources

CutOff Genes Podcast on Apple Podcasts—Ever wondered what consumer DNA testing can do for you—beyond telling you your ethnicity? Are you an adoptee—or someone who has an unknown parent or relative? Do you love Genealogy? You're in the right place. https://podcasts.apple.com/us/podcast/cutoff-genes-podcast

Hiraeth Hope and Healing—Providing retreats for adoptees, donor conceived people, late discovery adoptees, and NPEs. Hiraeth HopeandHealing.com

My Website—A complement to this book, my website includes articles, resources, podcast episodes, and much more about dealing with the NPE experiences. IamLezlee.com

NPE Friends Fellowship—Raising awareness by providing community and education to those affected by an NPE discovery. ihttps://npefellowship.org/g awareness by providing community and education to those affected by an NPE discovery.

References

https://www.iamlezlee.com.

"10 Things to Know about the Psychology of Ghosting." Online Psychology Degree Guide, October 1, 2021. https://www.online-psychologydegree.info/psychology-of-ghosting/.

Great Texas Land Rush. Accessed August 31, 2023. https://landrush.texasalmanac.com/.

Anderson, Steve. "Discover Your Ancestors in Obituaries ◆ Family-search." FamilySearch, August 5, 2022. https://www.familysearch.org/en/blog/discover-your-ancestors-in-obituaries.

Beattie, Melody. *Journey to the Heart: Daily Meditations on the Path to Freeing Your Soul*. HarperCollins Publishers, 2010.

"Best DNA Test Kits of 2023: Find the Best DNA Testing for Ancestry." www.top10.com, November 3, 2021. https://www.top10.com/dna-testing/comparison.

"Big Stick Ideology." Wikipedia, August 25, 2023. https://en.wikipedia.org/wiki/big_stick_ideology.

Brooks, Rob. "What Are the Chances That Your Dad Isn't Your Father?" *The Conversation*. January 31, 2023. https://theconversation.com/what-are-the-chances-that-your-dad-isnt-your-father-24802.

REFERENCES

Buchholz, Katharina, and Felix Richter. "Infographic: Consumer Genetic Testing Grows in Popularity." *Statista Daily Data.* November 18, 2019. https://www.statista.com/chart/19996/size-of-global-direct-to-consumer-gentic-testing-market/.

Emerald, Elizabeth. "The Right to Know?" *Medium.* May 16, 2022. https://medium.com/illumination/the-right-to-know-8b4390dcb669.

Gaille, Brandon. "30 Genetic Testing Industry Statistics and Trends." *BrandonGaille.com.* February 26, 2019. https://brandongaille.com/30-genetic-testing-industry-statistics-and-trends/.

Gilmore, Amy. "'What's in a Name?': Definition, Meaning, and Examples." Writing Tips. November 29, 2022. https://writingtips.org/whats-in-a-name/.

Huizen, Jennifer. "What Is Gaslighting? Examples and How to Respond." *Medical News Today.* July 14, 2022. https://www.medicalnewstoday.com/articles/gaslighting.

Lansford, Jennifer. "The Importance of Fathers for Child Development." *Psychology Today.* June 15, 2021. https://www.psychologytoday.com/us/blog/parenting-and-culture/202106/the-importance-fathers-child-development.

Lewis, Ricki. "DNA Day Has a New Meaning for Me This Year: I'm an NPE." *DNAScience.* May 18, 2020. https://dnascience.plos.org/2019/04/25/dna-day-has-a-new-meaning-for-me-this-year-im-an-npe/.

Liljenberg, Lezlee. *Genealogy: Uncovering Your Ancestry.* https://iamlezlee.com/.

McLeod, Danielle. "The Devil Is in the Details—Origin & Meaning." *GRAMMARIST.* January 20, 2023. https://grammarist.com/words/devil-is-in-the-details-vs-god-is-in-the-detail/.

Mercedes. "Beginner's Guide to Shared Centimorgans." *Who are You Made Of?*.February 3, 2023. https://whoareyoumadeof.com/blog/beginners-guide-shared-centimorgans.

Morton, Sunny. "Obituaries and Your DNA Matches." *Your DNA Guide—Diahan Southard.* July 5, 2022. https://www.yourdnaguide.com/ydgblog/obituaries-extend-your-family-tree.

Murphy, Heather. "What You're Unwrapping When You Get a DNA Test for Christmas." *New York Times.* December 22, 2019. https://www.nytimes.com/2019/12/22/science/dna-testing-kit-present.html.

Regalado, Antonio. "More than 26 Million People Have Taken an At-Home Ancestry Test." *MIT Technology Review.* June 18, 2020. https://www.technologyreview.com/2019/02/11/103446/more-than-26-million-people-have-taken-an-at-home-ancestry-test/.

"Rockabilly." *Encyclopædia Britannica.* July 27, 2023. https://www.britannica.com/art/rockabilly.

"Rockabilly." *Wikipedia.* August 24, 2023. https://en.wikipedia.org/wiki/rockabilly.

Sareea, Tanzeela. "10 Reasons You Should Never Consider Ghosting Someone." *Unwritten.* October 26, 2020. https://www.readunwritten.com/2017/02/14/10-reasons-never-consider-ghosting-someone/.

Schreiber, Stuart. "DNA Testing Leads Stuart Schreiber to Welcome Answers." Truth: A Love Story | *Harvard Magazine.* July 1, 2019. https://www.harvardmagazine.com/2019/06/dna-testing-schreiber#:~:text=A%20scientist%20discovers%20his%20own%20family's%20secrets.&text=Stuart%20Schreiber%20sits%20%E2%80%9Cwhere%20I,at%20Boston's%20Rose%20Kennedy%20Greenway.

Sturges, Eve. "Therapist, Writer, DNA Podcaster in Los Angeles." *EVE STURGES.* November 2, 2020. https://www.evesturges.la/.

Summer, Ivy. "How to Celebrate Father's Day: 25+ Fun & Easy Activities." WikiHow. March 18, 2023. https://www.wikihow.com/Celebrate-Father%27s-Day.

Unknown, Chris. "25 Best Metaphors for Life (That Will Inspire You!)." *Symbolism & Metaphor.* May 10, 2023. https://symbolismandmetaphor.com/metaphors-for-life/.

About the Author

LEZLEE LILJENBERG is a business owner, entrepreneur, and author on a mission to help others in the discovery of their true identities, their biological families and dealing with DNA surprises.

In a previous life Lezlee was a successful commercial real estate broker and in 2004 turned to insurance as she started her first agency from ground zero, growing the business to over $6 million in revenue in less than 12 years. After 18 years she sold her enterprise and formed Liljenberg Insurance Expert Witness, where she is a consultant and expert witness for insurance cases.

Over the past 30 years of her life, she knew there was something not quite right with comments and issues popping up concerning her past. Her DNA test from Ancestry sparked even more uncertainty in her heritage.

Lezlee spent several years asking all the right questions of her family and friends, to no avail. Then in 2020, her brother encouraged her to take the 23andMe test which would turn her life in a totally new, exciting, and, needles to say, a topsy turvy direction.

In 2021 she discovered the identity of her true biological family and has taken numerous steps to meet them, many times with disappointment and pain, but more importantly, she has encountered love and acceptance that overcomes the hurts. The uncertainty drives her forward and closer to the truth of the past and that of others.

Lezlee is sharing her DNA story about love, loss, pain and pursuit of the truth to hopefully help others know that they are not alone. Her story is not an unusual one as the community of the "Non-Parent Expected" grows exponentially every year.

She wholeheartedly believes that age should never keep you back from learning more and taking new adventures. No matter our age, ethnicity, origins or skin color we all are in this thing called "Life" together.

Lezlee Liljenberg holds a BA in Journalism/Public Relations and a MA in Political Science/Public Administration from the University of Texas at Arlington. Watch for her future publications, *Color Blind: Growing up to Never See the Color of Skin* and *The Birthday Girls: The Tale of a Female Tribe*. You can follow her blog and stay in touch with her at www.iamlezlee.com. She would love to hear your story and for you to become part of her family.

Made in the USA
Monee, IL
20 February 2024

53302726R00105